IN AND OUT OF FOCUS

Antoine L. Smith, Sr.

In and Out of Focus
Copyright © 2023 by Antoine L. Smith Sr.

All rights reserved. Published in the United States of America by Antoine L Smith Sr LLC in association with Jozef Syndicate, an imprint of Jozef PA of Louisiana LLC, P.O. Box 318013, Baton Rouge, LA 70831. www.jozefsyndicate.com

Cover design and manuscript editing by Antoinette Harrell.
The Library of Congress has established a Congress Control Number 2023908808 for this title. No part of this book may be reproduced or transmitted in any form or by any means without written permission from the author.

ISBN: 978-1-944155-35-3

ISBN: 978-1-944155-36-0 (ebook)

Alsmithsr@myyahoo.com
www.alsmithsr.com

Printed in the United States of America

DEDICATION

My parents, the Reverend Versay Smith and Hazel Holmes Smith, who both taught me the importance of staying focused as a child, are the inspirations behind this book. As a child, I was raised with a strong sense of responsibility and focus. A tremendous amount of value has been imparted to my life by my parents through the valuable lessons they taught me. There will always be a sense of gratitude in my heart for the life lessons I learned from them. There may have been times when I did not understand everything they were trying to tell me. It was through these experiences that my siblings and I learned what our parents tried to teach us throughout our early childhood development. With those lessons at heart, I dedicate this book in honor of their memory.

FORWARD

Dr. Antoinette Harrell
Author, Genealogist, and Louisiana Historian

The many projects I undertook and the number of books I've written have each required varied levels of focus. My greatest challenge is meeting tight deadlines, especially when I'm pressed for time. I have lost focus many times and sometimes couldn't regain it. While assisting Antoine with the writing of this book, I've learned how important it is to recognize when I am out of focus and what I can do to get back on track. At all costs, I learned how important it is to protect my focus.

Those who want to change their lives for the better or achieve a goal should read this book. You will gain a better understanding of yourself and of the habits that inhibit your focus. Additionally, you will be able to identify and change your bad habits. A situation arose while I was working on a project, and I quickly thought back to a few chapters from his book. Considering those chapters helped me gain a better understanding of where I was heading because, despite my best efforts, the mundane things of life kept getting in the way of my goal and purpose.

With this guide that you now hold, I learned how to balance those mundane things and stay focused. This book is designed for wealth-minded individuals who want to make intentional changes in their lives. By utilizing the self-reflections, this is a book that anyone can benefit from.

PREFACE

We all can lose focus, wander, and become distracted by the mundane things of life that can cause us to lose progress. Many people experience frustration because they cannot focus on their goals and purpose. As a result, they find it difficult to achieve their goals and purpose. This book was inspired by my desire to help others achieve or regain focus. Its purpose is to help you achieve your goals and accomplish the tasks that you set for yourself.

Over the course of my life, I have experienced ups and downs. It is true that I could have avoided some things if I hadn't been distracted or lost focus. I gained insight from listening to others share their problems, issues of life, and solutions with me.

As a child, my parents taught me the importance of staying focused at a very early age. In the years following the death of my father, I always felt as though I had gone from being a little boy and soon found myself stepping into manhood due to the immediate responsibilities I gained. It was a tumultuous time for us as a family, and every member of the family had to work hard to survive. I quickly learned that staying focused and staying dedicated are the keys to being successful in life. The other thing I learned was how getting out of focus can also have a negative impact at times. Ultimately, what you need to realize is that your life is not on autopilot. You have to manually set your focus. I've included questions at the end of each chapter to help you learn about yourself and what you need to change so that you are able to accomplish your true purpose.

TABLE OF CONTENTS

IN AND OUT OF FOCUS	1
DEDICATION	3
FORWARD	5
PREFACE	7
TABLE OF CONTENTS	9
WHAT IS FOCUS?	11
QUESTIONS	26
WHY SHOULD YOU STAY IN FOCUS?	27
QUESTIONS	46
HOW TO STAY FOCUS	48
QUESTIONS	57
PROTECTING YOUR FOCUS	58
QUESTIONS	66
THE POWER OF CONCENTRATION	67
QUESTIONS	75

THE POWER OF PRAYERS AND MEDITATION..76

QUESTIONS 87

GENERATIONAL FOCUS 89

QUESTIONS 101

DISTRACTIONS AND PROCRASTINATION 102

QUESTIONS 111

YOU ARE ON YOUR WAY 113

WHAT IS FOCUS?

Throughout my life, I have come to realize that focus is one of the most important things. Merriam-Webster's dictionary defines focus as the "act of paying close attention" to something. One must make sure that their attention is focused on what they are trying to accomplish in order for them to be successful. It is inevitable that we will lose focus from time to time, and we will undoubtedly lose focus when we lose concentration. In my childhood, I attended a series of lessons during Sunday School at church which helped me remain focused throughout the day. During the course of our study on focus, we spent a considerable amount of time going into depth about the subject. This is also where I learned the meaning of the word "mundane" for the first time.

My definition of focus is *to stay committed to what you are doing throughout the process*. It is inevitable in life that you will encounter challenges and triumphs, as well as setbacks, but you must remain focused in order to accomplish your goals or succeed in your tasks. If you want to achieve your goal, you must stay the course to the best of your ability. In the end, you will be happy with the result.

It could be said that all of us have some inclination that we are not focusing as we should. What are your methods of determining this? It becomes obvious when you are not working on your task or achieving your goals. The result is that you are out of focus, and it may be something that only you can recognize because you are out of focus. delay or an opportunity that has been missed because you did not do what you were supposed to do and you are aware of that. You lost focus somewhere along the way, so that you weren't able to achieve the goal you set. You might have heard people say, "if I had stayed in school", "if I had done this", or "if I had stayed with that, then I would have been promoted." They attest to the fact that if they had stayed the course, their success would have followed. It is important to keep in mind that getting off track is easy. Staying on track takes practice and plenty of it. As a result of your decision to stay in school or stay at your job, things might have turned out very differently.

It is a fact that no matter what our status is, how much wealth we possess, or what our material gains are, we must remain focused to succeed. I believe that's one of the reasons why I'm so passionate about writing this book. I want to assist you in staying focused in order to achieve the goal or task that you want to accomplish. Those who achieved anything in life did so by staying focused.

Taking a moment to reflect on my childhood, I was able to recall the chores I did as a child. I remember my mother telling me that in order for the household to run smoothly, everyone needed to do their part. In our household, structure played a very important role. The way my mother spoke to me when she was explaining something to me, was in a nice and calm voice, so that you could understand what she was saying. My mother wanted you to do the job right, so I had to stay focused on making sure I did it correctly. If I didn't do it right the first time, I made sure to do it right the second time, then I would not have to repeat the task a third or fourth time. As long as I stayed focused from the very beginning, it saved me a lot of time and effort in the end. As one of the many important lessons my mother taught me about structure, focus, and concentration, that is one of the most important.

As a child, I was responsible for helping my older siblings keep the younger children focused. This was considered one of the chores that they had to perform. My older siblings were positive examples for my younger siblings and me. We were all able to stay focused because we depended on each other for the function of our daily lives. Here is an example of what I did on a daily basis. We had to chop the wood and bring it indoors during the winter in order to keep the house warm. The fireplace had to be kept going as long as possible. In addition to cutting the grass, we also kept the house clean and tidy. It was never the case that girls were only responsible for washing and cooking in our house. It was my responsibility to wash clothes and clean with my brothers.

As a result of my early childhood lessons, I have been able to achieve success today. Our goal here is to teach you and assist you in training your mind so that you can stay focused on your tasks and goals and achieve them. It was because of our ability to stay focused that our household was functional. It was very important to my mother to have structure in how we operated as a family, and she taught my siblings and me the importance of structure from a very early age. As a child, Mama taught us the importance of following her instructions. It is for that reason that following instructions in my life right now is so important to me.

There was a particular time when I was in church listening to my cousin talk, and mama looked over and looked at me and my cousin. Just looking at us was enough to frighten me because I knew what that meant.

Early in my early childhood, I lost my father and we experienced a shift in our household. Consequently, it was my mother and two sisters who ran the house on a day-to-day basis. It was essential that we all kept our focus in order to survive. Without staying focused, we may have ended up homeless or faced other hardships. There has been no better way for my family to cope with the loss of my father than to go through it together. In addition to being a preacher, my father was also a farmer. The fact of the matter is, my mother didn't do any public work, in fact, she didn't even know what it was like to pay her bills. Everything was taken care of by my father. It was Mama who took care of the house and the children.

I am the sixth child in my family. It was the first time in my mother's life that she went to work after my father died. Her first job was at Sanderson's Farm, and she later worked at a plant nursery for a while. Besides this, she also did other odd jobs from time to time. I got my first job at the age of twelve. Although I was responsible for purchasing my own clothes, school supplies, and other items from my job, Mama never took a dime of the money I earned from my job. As a result, Mama has a little less financial burden to bear, which helps to lighten the load for her. Likewise, we had to make sure that we kept the household up and running in whatever way we could.

We did not experience any difficulties with our jobs interfering with our classes or schoolwork. We still had to complete our homework and maintain our focus in the classroom as Mama had instructed us to do. In terms of time, we didn't waste any time so to speak. We knew what we had to do and we just got it done. In the end, there was plenty of time left for us to play. The problem was that we had other things to do. It was important for us to remain focused in order to complete the tasks. Many of you have memories quite similar to mine of all the times when you as a child or as a teen had focus to accomplish chores or school assignments—even the most mundane ones.

As we go through the everyday routines of our lives, we tend to lose focus on the important things in life. In the same way that there are days when I didn't want to go to church or to work, there were days when I did not want to go to school. It is easy to get tired of doing the same thing over and over again every day. When the mundane aspects of life get to you, it can be very easy for you to become overwhelmed or even unbothered. Nevertheless, it is important that you keep your focus because you have a spouse to take care of, children to rear and guide, a church to attend, and many other duties and responsibilities to take care of. The fact that someone is relying on you is a very humbling experience. The most important thing is to stay focused, even if you can't see the end result.

Take a moment and consider these questions. What do you think is the reason you are not focusing on what you should be doing? What are some of the signs that you are out of focus?

Let me share a unique thought with you. Do you know it is possible to keep the *maximum* focus to a *minimum* in order to ensure *maximum* effectiveness? What are your thoughts on this?

The point I want to make here is that if you increase your focus, you will achieve maximum results. What methods do you use to increase your focus? If you want to create a plan of action, you need a method that will help you to create a pattern of focus in order to achieve your goal.

Do you feel that you are achieving your goals? Do you achieve the goal you set for yourself? If so, why are you achieving it? In any and all cases, why aren't you achieving the goals you have set for yourself? Is it possible for you to distinguish between being in focus and being out of focus? The focus is on you, so let's go back to you for a moment.

What type of person do you consider yourself to be? A procrastinator or a person who endeavors to complete the task at hand with the utmost, maximum effort no matter what the circumstances in their lives may be?

There is a responsibility on your shoulders. Neither education, job status, community status, or church status has anything to do with this. The focus was lost somewhere, which resulted in all hope being lost. The key to staying focused is for you to learn how to do it. In order for the president to be able to do his job effectively, he must stay focused. There is a finger pointing at you from within these pages. This book is intended for the individual who is reading it: you!

In the great words of Michael Jackson, the work ahead is "starting with the man in the mirror". That is what this book is about: looking in the mirror and starting with a look at yourself.

As you look into the mirror, you will see yourself completely. It is up to you to determine your level of focus, no one else can do that for you. With where you are now, what is your level of focus like? What is the level of focus you would like to have? What is the maximum level of focus needed for you to accomplish your goals?

I am aware of what I have been taught Biblically about the importance of focus. Remember, due to the loss of focus, the children of Israel wandered for forty years in the wilderness before reaching the Promise Land.

Don't lose focus! Keep your eyes on the prize! It is important to know when things aren't going according to your plan, because this is a sign that you are out of focus. Everyone knows when they are out of focus because the negative results indicate it. For those who are staying focused, they are being rewarded with positive results.

You will quickly be able to tell whether you are at maximum or minimum focus. The difference can be seen in your accomplishments. This may sound simple, but the way you know you are not focused is when you are not achieving what you should be achieving. You will learn how to stay focused with the help of this book.

There are a lot of things that can distract us from what needs to be done. There are some issues in life that cannot be avoided, but you must get your focus in order to succeed. Our society today is faced with the distraction of social media and this is one of the many problems with which we are dealing. It is important to consider how much time you can spend on social media sites. Whether you are a youth or an adult, you can spend endless hours unintentionally strolling around on social media websites. Spending time on things that you shouldn't be focusing on takes quality time away from what really needs to be done.

There is no doubt that social media can take a lot of time from your family, your work, your studies, and most importantly, from you as an individual. The problem is that you are not able to focus on what you are doing. I am certain that if you are reading this book, staying focused is one of your major concerns. If you are one of the people who spends a lot of time on the internet, watching movies, or chatting online when you should be completing an application for a position or attending class or even starting your own business, then you may be one of those people who use minimum and no focus. The truth is, everybody has an idea as to whether they are in focus or out of focus.

This book can be seen as a manual and a guide that everyone can benefit from. We can all learn how to stay focused and how important it is that you pay attention to your goals at all times. This book is intended for every reader to be able to identify their shortcomings and become equipped with a plan to maximize their focus as needed.

As I write this, I am 100% focused, and it is helping me in many ways. I was informed by the person who is assisting me with writing the book that it is allowing her to stay focused on her projects and on the various responsibilities and projects in her life that matter most to her.

There is no doubt that this is one of my many dreams. In fact, the idea for this book has been brewing in my head for ten years and I have always been determined to see it through. Now, a decade later, I was able to write and publish my first book. A second book is on my bucket list and I can't wait to get started.

Having experienced the consequences of not being focused, I know it can lead to major delays, failures, disappointments, and separations. It is important to maintain focus regardless of the issue at hand. Although there are different causes and situations, the end result remains the same if you are not focused. It is when people stop focusing on their goals that they become failures, lose their family, lose their jobs, lose money, or lose their lives. The lack of focus has led to some people giving up and not being able to find their way again.

The other day, I was thinking about how easily we can lose focus when we are not paying attention to our goal. It could be a matter of helping another person or managing a personal issue that you could not avoid. There is no doubt that these things will occur. The question you need to ask yourself is how can I regain focus? Am I going to let the issue get in the way of my progress? Will I use that as an excuse?

Whether you are a staff member of the White House, or a homeless person, a student, a parent, a leader, or just a regular individual. It is common for all of us to lose focus from time to time. In one of the verses in the Bible that tells us not to be weary in doing good, it says not to be weary in doing good. When you are concentrating on what you are doing, it is sometimes easy to get caught up in what you are doing.

> *Let us not become weary in doing good, for at the proper time we will reap a harvest if we do not give up.*
>
> *Galatians 6:9*

My favorite scripture is in Joshua the first chapter when God tells Joshua, "My servant Moses is dead, but as I was with Moses, I will be with you as well." Joshua witnessed God do the same thing to Moses, so I know He can do the same for me. Joshua only had to remain focused, and God would take care of the rest. I find Psalm 23, "The Lord is my shepherd," to be one of my favorite scriptures. It builds my faith to believe that God will take care of me as long as I remain focused. Remember, the Promised Land was offered as a reward for the children of Israel following God's instructions. It remains God's promise to us that He will never leave us or fail us. It was not clear to them that they would succeed in the end, but maintaining focused on God was essential. During Sunday School lessons, I took mental pictures of everything God said in His Word. To remain focused, one must take the first step.

Inevitably, there will always be problems in life. It is necessary to learn how to deal with and process these situations without allowing them to keep breaking your focus. In life, sometimes some things happen that help us to stay focused on what needs to be done. In order to achieve your goal, the most important thing is to recognize that situations and distractions can be stepping stones.

We all go through ups and downs in our lives. It is important to recognize that some of those down things may help us to see new paths and strategies for success. Our ability to redirect ourselves is something we learn over time and with every setback. You will have some days that are harder than others, but if you stay focused and do not fall into the negative distractions, you will be fine. You can experience life in a way that can set you back a little bit but don't allow it to get the best of you. Remember this next time you face an adversary. Get back to being focused. Storms are a part of life, but calm follows. The road to success will be full of challenges and tribulations, but you just have to fight harder to remain focused.

Despite the fact that the clouds are low, you can focus on the fact that the sun will rise soon.

> *"For our present troubles are small and won't last very long. Yet they produce for us a glory that vastly outweighs them and will last forever! So, we don't look at the troubles we can see now; rather, we fix our gaze on things that cannot be seen. For the things we see now will soon be gone, but the things we cannot see will last forever.*
>
> *2 Corinthians 17-18*

There is no going back on God's Word. It brought to mind an incident that occurred in 1983 when there was a severe rainstorm with low clouds and lots of rain. It felt like forty days and forty nights, and the rain didn't stop. Despite all, the sun shined. Bobby, a friend, said, Smith, the sun is still shining. The clouds are hanging, and the sun has blacked out. You will see a silver line once the cloud is over and the sun is shining. The sun reappeared after several days. Stay focused and you'll succeed. Everything will be fine.

In another example, I was talking with my son one Sunday during church. He was a senior in high school questioning if he was wasting his time. His school activities, Upward Bound programs, and church programs kept him away from playing with the boys. I answered, "Dad will tell you this. You may not be wasting your time. You won't accomplish your goals if you stop now. Stop now and you'll waste time." Currently, he is vice president of Crown Royal Whiskey Company in Illinois. Across the United States, he covers five states and multiple plants. Choosing to stay focused on all these important activities paid off and led him down a path of success.

Focus is a result of choices that are made at an early age. There is a price associated with having too much freedom in terms of what one chooses to do. An old saying states, "Don't give him too much rope.". He will hang himself if you give him too much rope. Keep an eye on everything. Be careful how much rope you give yourself.

The most important thing is to set boundaries and to stay within them as much as possible. In order to be successful, you need to have boundaries and timelines in place otherwise, you won't be able to achieve your goals. The line can easily be crossed if you are not careful. It is important to remember that every successful person has a boundary. It is an example of a boundary for me to be between 7:00 p.m. and 9:00 p.m. I am asleep in my bed. It is my nature to wake up early in the morning. Every Sunday at 9:00 a.m., I am walking into the church doors for service. As far as I am concerned, I know what it takes for me to accomplish what I need to do. The ability to stay focused is something that I learn and practice each and every day. In our discussion about staying focused, we discussed the need to find a way back if you fall off focus. You cannot simply jump back on course, you have to create a plan to get yourself back on track.

In order to make sure that this isn't misconstrued as something that should be blamed on anyone or anything else, it is important to stress that being focus is a personal issue. As I look at myself, I am thinking to myself as I look at myself. We are in the habit of pointing out what others have done to cause us to fail. What do I do? I'm not sure, but something needs to be done. Each individual must see what he or she is doing or not doing. Yes, that's correct. No one else will be responsible but you.

For you to get where you desire to go, you have to not only take the right steps but you must take intentional, focused steps. The only person who can do what it takes to get there is you. The problem is that you feel you are already behind schedule when it comes to being where you most desire. It is very easy to point the finger at others than to point the finger at yourself. I intend to get you to look within yourself in order to achieve your goal. As you continue through this book, use my experiences and the questions throughout to discover yourself, your habits, and how you operate. Through the experience of writing this book, I am now able to tell you that I understand what it takes to be a focused writer. There were weekly meetings with the editor every Friday that I had to attend. Regardless of how long it took us to complete the task, I had to stay focused. There was no doubt in my mind that I would fulfill my dream.

When you are focused and fully concentrating, you have a goal-driven mindset. You have blocked out all kinds of distractions, and you have learned how to balance life so that you can accomplish the task at hand. You have a clear idea of what you want to accomplish. You know you have to stay at home and study or work on your business plan for the next few hours. It is also possible to simply spend time with your family, or whatever else you wish to achieve if that is what you desire. There might be a reason for this, such as trying to pay off your credit card bills as quickly as possible. Whether you don't have the money to travel, go out, or eat out, you realize that you cannot afford it.

For example, I recently purchased a tractor and wanted to pay it off as soon as possible. It was my responsibility to work overtime at my job to earn extra money for the principle so I could pay it back. Nevertheless, being focused on that goal was necessary.

If I were to sum up what I am saying here, I would say that if you stay focused on what you need to accomplish in your life, your goal will be achieved. That's the point I'm trying to make here, and that's what I'm trying to say. If you do not stay focused on your goal, you will not be able to achieve it. As soon as you fail to stick to the plan that was set forth, it is so easy for you to lose focus on what you should be doing. It is important to note that if you are trying to lose weight and you are eating the same foods that are making you gain weight, then you are not exercising. It is clear to you what you are not doing. You may be interested in writing a book, but you have not yet written your first sentence.

As a result of all the how-tos available in this day and age, you have no reason to think that you will not be able to accomplish your goals. You may have stopped to consider the fact that you are not applying yourself to your job because you are not focused on it. It is also possible that you may have mentioned that being out of focus contributed to the fact that you failed. In the event you are not focused, the consequences can be catastrophic. When you are in focus, you are talking about the outcome, whereas if you are out of focus, you are talking about what did not happen, so it is important to understand this. Keep your focus on the task at hand. The bottom line is that you have to be able to focus on what you are doing.

At the end of the day, you are still trying to achieve your goal, no matter if you succeed or fail. Can you say that you are successful? This book is all about helping you become the best version of yourself that you can be. Keep your focus on what you are doing at all times. I want to be clear here, it is time to meet the man who is looking back at you in the mirror. Could that person in the mirror commit to achieving the goal he or she has set for themselves? Are you willing to learn how to stay focused and to learn how to stay on task?

QUESTIONS

1. What does focus mean to you? _____
   _____
   _____

2. Do you think that you need to work on being focused? _____
   _____

3. What is taking you out of focus? _____
   _____
   _____

4. What habits do you need to change to get in focus? _____
   _____
   _____

5. How long do you stay in focus? _____
   _____
   _____

6. How long do you stay out of focus? _____
   _____

7. Do you have a method that can help you get back in focus?
   _____
   _____

8. Do you think you can accomplish your goal with minimum focus?
   _____
   _____

WHY SHOULD YOU STAY IN FOCUS?

Staying focused on your goal or task is one of the most important things you can do to achieve success. There is no doubt that you will be successful in accomplishing that mission in the end. Allowing yourself to lose focus will cause you to become distracted, and that will cause you to stress and delay you in accomplishing your goal if you let it.

When you get out of focus, there is a price you will have to pay, and only you can determine how much that price will be. As for your outcome, it will be determined by whether you are in focus or out of focus. It is important to keep in mind that you are the only one who can determine the outcome of the situation. Imagine that you were taking a picture of a nature scene or a person, for example. You are looking into the camera and you are not using the auto mode on the camera, so you have to focus it manually since you are not using the auto mode on the camera. The image can become blurry and out of focus if the settings are not correct. You can apply the same concept to your goals and tasks as well.

I think you should determine what you have to lose by getting out of focus and what you have to gain by staying focused. It would be a good idea for you to write down what you have to lose, and then write down what you have to gain so that you can better determine why you should stay focused. You should read it out every day for a few days and concentrate on what you wrote down. There is never a moment when I am not carrying my black book with me at all times. It is for many reasons that I write in my book every day. To stay focused on my tasks, I find it helpful to write them down. You need to put some order in your life so that you can be focused on what needs to be done. Based on my own experience, I hope that my experience will be able to assist you in your efforts to achieve your goal. I need to write it down, otherwise, things can get out of hand and overwhelmed.

It is easy for me to find myself all over the place, not achieving anything. As you will see throughout my book, the structure is one of the most important aspects, and it has been written several times throughout that structure, distractions, and focus are all prominent parts of the book that are discussed in great detail.

It is only you who can decide what the result will be in the end, and it is only you who can make that decision. There is no need for you to worry if you are working on a project or if you want to reach a particular goal that you are aiming for. The thing to remember is that as long as you're happy with what you're doing, it doesn't matter what you're doing. There is no doubt that staying focused on what you are doing is one of the keys to success. Everyone can lose focus from time to time and there is a possibility that it will happen to you. It is a challenge for many people to stay focused on what they are doing at any given time. At some point in our lives, we will all cross the path of getting out of focus, since it is inevitable that we will all do so at some point in our lives. In the end, only you will be able to determine the outcome of the situation.

I would like to tell you a little bit about myself. After I had an affair, I got out of focus, and as a result, I lost my wife. From my upbringing and the lessons I learned in church, I knew that having an affair was not the right thing to do. Upon learning that my wife was having an affair, I allowed my emotions to get the better of me and lost focus, which led to the same things I did when I learned that she was having an affair. The answer to the question is no, it was not the right thing for me to do. There was no reason for me to let what someone else did take my focus away from what I needed to do. It didn't make it right in my case because two wrongs didn't make it right. Due to the lack of focus on my part, I got divorced as a result. I had to pay that price for getting out of focus.

The next thing I would like to talk about is what I was able to accomplish by standing in focus. Throughout my career, I worked for one electrical company for 36 years. Following my retirement from the company, I started my own business. A major goal of mine was to open my own business one day. It was very important for me to stay focused on what I wanted to do after I retired. A few years ago, when I was watching Bishop T.D. Jakes on television. He said that if you are working for someone, stay focused, learn everything you can, and save money so that one day you will be able to open your own business.

My childhood is one of my favorite memories and I would like to go back there. I dreamed of becoming a truck driver when I was a little boy, and I dreamed of owning my truck. I was informed by my youngest brother Clyde one day that the coach at the school had a job for me that I would be interested in. It was decided that I would meet with the coach and discuss the job with him. I had my first job at Louisiana Power and Light when I was nineteen years old and starting my career in the electrical industry. The truth is, I didn't know anything, and I didn't even know why I had been selected for this particular position. It was the first time that a black person was hired to do this job in Amite, Louisiana.

The reason I was so determined to keep my focus was that I was taking a close look at everything the job had to offer, and I did not want to lose sight of it. Here is what I had to lose if I didn't stay focused on what I needed to accomplish. It is likely that I would have lost a job that paid more money and had more benefits like medical, 401K, retirement, and many other benefits that come with the job. To make sure all these benefits were kept for my family and me, I was going to remain focused. It was important for me to be on time at work and to make the most of my learning experience. On the job, I knew that I was not going to be distracted by anything that was going on around me. There was too much I had to protect and too much I had to let loose.

No matter what is going on in your life, you need to bring yourself back to your focus. It is very important that you do not allow anything or anyone to cause you to lose focus. The first thing you need to understand is that they do not see your dreams, goals, and purposes. Consequently, they are not going to protect your focus, it is all up to you, just remember that. Only you can stop you, no one else can do it for you. In the end, it comes back to the person who is looking in the mirror.

We all know how long we can stay focused on something. The ability to stay focused is a challenge for some people. Some people find it difficult to sit down for ten minutes and read a book on their own. Others may find it easier to stay focused than others. The problem of not being able to stay focused can be a result of a medical condition for some, while for others, staying focused on the task is something they have no choice but to do. In my experience, I have seen many people with physical disabilities become well-known artists over the years. In some cases, they may not be able to use their hands at all, or they may not even have any hands to use. Using their mouths, they can draw and paint. There was a lady I saw who had no arms or hands and was cooking dinner with her feet while she was without any arms or hands. Are you aware of how much concentration and focus they require to achieve the goals and tasks they have set for themselves? It became clear to them why it was so important to stay focused throughout the process.

It was up to them whether they worked with what they had or not. Their understanding was that if they wanted to get what they needed, they had to stay focused in order to be able to accomplish it. There is no way you will be able to accomplish anything without being focused in some way. When I was trying to start my own business, I needed to take care of some things like applying for occupational licenses, which are registered with the State of Louisiana. My goal-oriented nature and refusal to allow anything or anyone to distract me helped me to stay focused and achieve this goal.

There will always be distractions around you, so it is important to always remember that. As a matter of fact, you can't avoid it in life. Your response to the situation is entirely up to you. As we all know, there will be many challenges and disappointments as we go through life. It is up to you to decide how you will respond to the situation. Is it going to take you out of focus if you allow it to happen?

The way I lived my life has been governed by my parents teaching us to stick together no matter what happened. As I progressed in life, I discovered that even in my family I had to set boundaries. If I did not set the boundaries, I would lose focus and the stakes would be too high for me to ignore them. I couldn't continue lending money, since they were interfering with my personal time. Money was not as important to me as my time was. As the saying goes, "Time is money, and money is time, and time is money. There was a need to protect my time, my focus, and my money at the same time. As I grew up, I learned that my family's habits are not the same as mine. In later life, after I became an adult, I realized that we are all individuals, and I learned that the hard way.

There is no doubt that we are all confronted with the game of life and may or may not understand the game of life. When I listened to Earl Nightingale speak about "Stop Doing What Poor People Do", he stated that ninety-five percent of people do not see success, and only five percent of people become successful. Basically, what he is telling us is that we have to make up our minds about what we are going to do. If you want to achieve the goal and accomplish the task that you have set for yourself, you will need to make up your mind about it.

If you want to accomplish something, you have to define exactly what it is that you want to accomplish. Decide what you want to achieve and then go after it with boldness. Is your compass pointing in the right direction? Do you feel that your compass is guiding you in the right direction?

There is a price tag attached to losing focus, and it may be too high for you to afford. You are planning to take the classes needed to get your master's degree, but you haven't even started working on the process of getting your degree yet. Have you ever found yourself putting off doing something you want to do for years on end? There is a problem preventing you from focusing on your work. What is keeping you from focusing on your work and what can you do to fix it? There is one thing I want to point out, you have to do something different if you want to get a different result. If you keep going the same way, you will get the same results if you keep doing the same thing. There is a good chance that the compass will always lead you back in the same direction. There will be a change in the compass when you change your direction.

During my early years, I learned a great deal from watching my parents and other adults in the community where I was raised. The two of them were very responsible people and worked very hard to provide for the needs of their families. In order to achieve their goals, they set boundaries for themselves. It was from them that I learned how to set boundaries and goals, as well as how important it was to set those goals. Staying focused is one of the most important things that I have learned so far. I had to save my money and purchase my school clothes when I was a young boy working to buy my school clothes. When I was a young boy, I often took my money with me to the store when I went to the store. My money couldn't be spent on anything in the store since. To pay for school clothes and lunch money, I had to save the money to pay for them.

No matter how tempted I was to purchase items like those of the other children, I had to stay focused and not let myself be tempted. My mother used to save all the money I earned from working after I went home from work. The money would be put up by my mother and in August, I would go to Sears and Roebuck's catalog and order my clothes from them.

As soon as the brown paper bag with my name on it came to our house, I knew it was for me. The mere sight of that box was enough to make me so excited. There was no doubt in my mind that I was ready to start school in September. When I was a child, I stayed focused on what I had to do. There was a goal I set for myself, and I achieved it. As a matter of fact, this was one of the first lessons I learned about accountability. Throughout the process, I learned several important lessons that I will be able to apply in the future.

There are times when it is difficult to focus. We will inevitably all come to learn that sooner or later. Everyone needs to work on being more focused in their daily lives. Being focused requires a lot of time and effort on your part. It is very important to remain focused and concentrate on your goal if you want to achieve it. It is important that you follow through with it. The cost of staying focused can be very rewarding in the end. Make sure that you are alert to what is happening and that you do not get involved in things that do not pertain to or concern you in any way.

Keeping focus is one of the most important lessons you should learn as early as possible if you want to succeed in your goals or tasks. If you ask yourself why you should remain focused, you will find the answer. You won't regret learning how to remain focused and why it is so important for you to stay focused. Each and every one of us had a reason for staying focused. What are the goals that you are trying to achieve? How do you plan on achieving the goals you have set for yourself? How can you overcome a big obstacle? Can you give a brief explanation of why you find it important to stay focused?

Oftentimes, the biggest obstacle that stands in the way of your goals is you. Yourself. Many obstacles can arise as a result of a lack of focus. Many of us can attest to allowing something or someone to distract us from what we are doing or working on. Throughout this book, you will learn how to identify distracting factors and how to stay focused on what you are doing. When you are studying for an exam, and you are preparing for an exam, and you have an unexpected guest come over to chat for a few minutes while you're studying for an exam, that would be a great example. As you are probably aware, you need to study in order to pass any exam. As a result, you allowed them to break your concentration on things or people that don't have anything to do with you. Due to this, you did not have enough time to study. As a result of the exam, you did not score very well. Who is to blame for that? Regardless of whether you succeed or fail, you are the only one who can determine your fate. It is understandable that you would like to spend some time with her. It was just not the right time to do it now. It was very important for you to study for your exams.

On the job, I was learning to pace myself and stay focused so that I didn't lose time while working. It was very important for me to stay focused in order not to lose too much time or energy. My productivity was protected by me. It wasn't long after I finished the task that I was able to take a break and enjoy my favorite drink, Gatorade. My goal was to be productive rather than to be the fastest, so I stayed focused on that. That is what works best for me. Neither time nor energy was wasted. What I am trying to say is that I did not stop and I stayed focused on what I was doing. It was important for me to stay focused throughout the process. As you read the book, you will hear me emphasize over and over again how important it is to stay focused on your goals. Obviously, this is the subject matter of the book, correct?

I suggest that you channel your focus onto that which you would like to accomplish. To achieve self-mastery over your thoughts, and to constantly direct your time towards your goals and objectives is what Napoleon Hill says in his book Think and Grow Rich. Focus on the goals you want to achieve and find ways to accomplish those goals by putting your attention on them and finding ways to accomplish them. Achieving or not attaining your goal is up to you alone. Only you can decide if you are going to achieve it or not. Therefore, it is important to put into action a plan of action. You need to identify your distractions and get back on track if you want to stay focused.

There is no doubt that writing down your plan and your goals will help you achieve them. It would also be a good idea to write down how you plan to accomplish those goals. The process by which you plan on achieving that goal should be outlined in some detail. As a result, you will be able to stay focused. In my life, it has helped me accomplish many goals and tasks that I have set for myself. It is very unlikely that I would be successful if I didn't write down my goals and plans in advance. In my practice of thirty-six years, this has always been the way I work. Several decades ago, when I first started working for Louisiana Power & Light Co., one of my supervisors told me that I was supposed to know how to do something that I had no experience with when I first started working there. After that day, I learned that if I wanted to remember something, I had to write it down. The practice of writing things down has remained with me to this very day.

The very important thing that I am trying to point out here is that writing down your goals is one of the most powerful things you can do for yourself. To clarify your goals, you will need to write them down as well as the tasks you wish to accomplish. It is important to study successful people if you want to achieve success. Everybody has dreams, and everyone has goals, but how many of them are actually able to achieve those goals? The second step after you have dreamed of your dream is to write down your goals. Let us take a look at a successful business person as an example. It is obvious to that person that a business plan is necessary. Having obtained the business plan, the company can now present the plan to the banker and investors for their review once they have obtained the plan. In other words, what are their goals? As far as they are concerned, they want the banker as well as the investors to invest in their business. Business plans are one of the keys to a company's success, and they are essential to its success. It is up to you to unlock the door and you have the key in your hand. You are capable of achieving your full potential. Put your plan into action by writing it down and putting it into action. You will be able to remain focused if you have a well-written plan.

Your success is determined by your ability to stay focused, and your failure is determined by your inability to stay focused. That's all there is to it. There will be a direct correlation between it and the outcome of your project. In this chapter, we will provide you with a few examples that will help you to understand why staying focused is so important. Staying focused can be very powerful if you keep your eyes on the prize. Once your mind is trained to stay focused, you will be able to do that more easily in the future. Staying focused is one of the most important concepts that you will learn during this course. While it may seem difficult at first, if you practice focusing, it will become a daily part of your life as it will become a habit. Mind control is one of the most important skills that you should learn.

The act of writing down your plan gives you direction and structure. By doing so, you can outline the order in which tasks need to be accomplished. There is no doubt that this will help you to stay focused. We all know how our minds can wander all over the place as human beings, so we don't have to worry about it. By writing down your thoughts, it helps your mind to remain focused. Putting your thoughts down on paper has a great deal of power. There is only so much that your mind can hold at one time. I think we all have the tendency to forget some very important things from time to time. So, if you want to be successful, don't depend on your mind alone. You can get off focus just by focusing on the mundane things that happen every day. When you write it down, it can be a great way to help you refocus on your goal to achieve it. In the end, you will see positive results and you will look forward to writing down your tasks and accomplishing them as soon as possible.

Regardless of what the situation is, there is always a way out. It is imperative that you remain focused at all times. It was at the age of twelve that I learned how important it is to focus. I had a clear vision of what I wanted to achieve, so I set my mind to it. I was able to save money all week long and buy my school clothing and school supplies after working all week long and working hard all week long. As soon as school started and I had all my school clothing and school supplies, I was happy that I stayed focused and stayed focused on my studies. In fact, I was able to learn how to set more goals for myself and work hard to achieve those goals. This was a huge undertaking for a young boy who was only twelve years old.

As a father, I passed the same practices and work ethic on to my son, Antoine Jr. The first time he earned his own money was when he was just five years old. It was twenty-five dollars a yard when he started cutting grass. His second job was to clean the Lodge Hall, and for twenty-five dollars a month, I was teaching him the basics of how to do the work. His tithes were paid from his pocket at the church out of his own money. It was my duty to teach him the importance of work ethic and saving his money at the same time. Years later, the lessons I was taught have paid off in a big way. Currently, he has achieved a great deal of success in his life. The point I am trying to make is that it is never too early for these lessons to be taught to children. You must focus on what you want to achieve and go after it with all your mind, body, and soul.

What do I mean when I say that everything inside of you is important? There is no doubt in my mind that you have what it takes inside of you. There are times when we just need someone to help point us in the right direction when we are unsure where to go. In the world of business, there is a scripture that states, "Iron sharpens iron". In my experience, I find that when I surround myself with positive-thinking people, I am able to stay focused and concentrate on my goal. It helped me to enhance my focus by listening to motivational audio books or speakers. I learned a lot from them.

Across the world, millions of people go to work every day and stay focused on their work. Having obligations to keep is one of the things that they are aware of. There is no doubt that they are aware of the fact that they have to provide for their families. Therefore, that is the reason why they remain focused on their work. Defining the reason for staying focused is up to you. It is impossible to achieve anything worthwhile without a strong focus. When you do something as simple as do the laundry, prepare dinner, maintain the lawn, etc., you have to focus on it in order to get the job done. Whether the task is small or large, it doesn't matter how big or how small it is.

In this chapter, we have discussed the benefits of being in focus. Now that the benefits of being in focus have been discussed, we can now discuss the effects of not being in focus. As I mentioned earlier about the laundry, the lawn, and preparing dinner, I have been very busy. As we all know, if you do not do your laundry, you will have an overabundance of dirty clothes when you do not do your laundry. The yard will grow out of control and the family won't have anything to eat in the evening as a result. All of us get tired of doing the same things over and over again on a daily and weekly basis. The fact remains that in order to maintain our daily lives, we must accomplish certain tasks and maintain a daily routine. Despite being tired, we still get the chores done because we don't want the laundry to pile up, the yard to become untidy, and our neighbors to start complaining about it. Certainly, we do not want hungry kids to cry because they are hungry. In order to eliminate those problems, we will do whatever it takes to make it happen. "Why?" We should be doing these tasks because as you know, if we do not, it will cost us a lot of money."

You will indeed have to have a made-up mind before you start. The best example I can give here is that of Jesus Christ. It was Christ's goal to do the works that his Heavenly Father asked him to do. There was no way he was going to let himself be distracted by things of this world. His focus remained on spreading the good news of his father to as many people as possible. It was important for him to remain focused to keep his mind on what he needed to accomplish. When it comes to staying focused, Christ is the perfect example to follow. That is why we must stay focused to accomplish our tasks daily. To accomplish our daily goals, we must perform the mundane tasks of life that make up our daily lives.

Why are you trying to accomplish what you are trying to accomplish? There is no doubt that I wanted to write this book to serve as a guide for you. How did I go about accomplishing that? What was the process I had to follow? Every Friday, at 9:30 a.m., I meet with Dr. Antoinette Harrell and work for hours on end. During that time, I had no choice but to put everything else aside. I can assure you that I am telling the truth. For my company, I also had a number of other important tasks that had to be completed. Multi-tasking was something I was doing at the time. While I was on my break, I called my employees to let them know what was happening. As I was on my lunch break, I called the employees to find out how they were doing. In the course of my break, I checked my e-mails. During the hours that we were working, I could not allow myself to be distracted by anything else during those hours.

There was no doubt in my mind that I was going to use my own book as a guide. It was important for me to stay focused to write this book in order to provide you with help. I am sharing my own experience with you that I have gained over the years. I managed to remain focused on my goal of becoming an author, and a motivational speaker. It was my goal to help someone find focus in their lives. This is the reason why I found it so important to remain focused during this time.

In this chapter, I will talk about the mundane things of life that can't be avoided in life and those things that can be avoided. I would now like to turn my attention to the things that can be avoided, so let's start with them.

During the birth of a baby, the umbilical cord is cut from the mother in order to separate the baby from the mother. In my opinion, you must learn how to separate yourself from the negativity that surrounds you. It is possible to lose focus if you are surrounded by people who are not like-minded. Let me give you an example of what I mean. If you have a friend who likes to go out on the weekends and sometimes during the week, you may enjoy going out with her. The friend is always talking about what is happening at the clubs or other social gatherings around town. There is no point in letting their actions distract you from what you want to achieve in your life. They have no interest in talking to you about anything concerning your project, so there is no point in trying to talk to them about it. The only thing they are interested in talking about is what is happening in the clubs at the moment. There is no doubt that this is a major distraction to you. This is what I refer to as a negative distraction that can be avoided.

Regarding negative distractions, I would like to make a few points. In a recent conversation with Dr. Antionette Harrell, we discussed how important it is to stay focused when you are preparing to speak at a conference or a meeting. As I arrived early to set up, I was focused on my presentation, and then someone approaches me and tries to talk to me about something that has absolutely nothing to do with what I am going to talk about. It is getting closer to the time when you will be able to speak, so you need to tell that person that you must remain focused on your task at hand. Obviously, that is a negative distraction and if you wish to be successful in fulfilling your task, you will have to learn how to deal with negative distractions like these.

I hope that in this chapter, you will learn about the importance of staying focused and what will happen to you if you don't stay focused. You will find at the end of this chapter several questions that only you are capable of answering. As you answer the question, you will have the opportunity to analyze what gets you out of focus and what you can do to improve your focus. It is important that you answer each question honestly and carefully. Unless you do that, you will never be able to correct the situation.

I know that this book has been inside of me for at least ten years now. Throughout my life, I have never lost sight of my desire to write my own book. It was just a matter of finding someone who could assist me in making my dream a reality. In my opinion, that was my third step in the process. I began my writing journey with the desire to write a book as my first step. The second step I took was to start writing. Over the years, I have been writing a lot. The final point I would like to make is that while doing some electrical work at the home of Dr. Harrell, I heard her talking about the book she recently published. This gave me the chance to talk to her about my book and ask her if she would be able to assist me with it. My book was in my mind when I was working on the job and I didn't hesitate to talk with her about direction when I was working on the job. The point I am trying to make is that I was so focused on writing my book. The desire to write and publish my first book among others remains the same ten years later, and I never lose sight of the desire to do so. If I had given up on my dreams of becoming an author because it took me ten years to achieve them, what would have happened to me? It's important to keep in mind that a delay does not mean that your application has been denied.

Throughout the years, I have spoken with many people, including Rev. Lafitte Tucker, about this book. He was inspirational to me. "The conversations I have been having with Antoine about staying focused have helped me in my personal life," Rev. Tucker said. He has been one of my biggest cheerleaders and motivators throughout my life. In the last few days, I have been receiving calls from him about how he is staying focused. As a matter of fact, this is a conversation that is often had between the two of us. The fire inside me was kept burning by this. As I was helping him, he was also helping me in return. There was a reciprocal feeding of energies going on between us.

In fact, Dr. Harrell told me on many occasions that this topic of being in and out of focus has helped her stay on track with her projects so much so that she looked forward to working with me on Fridays. Take a moment to let that sink in for a moment. It is interesting to see that here is a person who has written a few books, produced films, and she is telling me how my book has helped her in her work.

The point that I am trying to make here is no matter where you are in life, everyone needs to learn how to stay focused, no matter what their situation is. No matter who you are, whether you are a person on the street or a person in the White House, we all face the same challenges when it comes to remaining focused. You can do it, if I can do it.

It is very important that you find someone who is like-minded, who is passionate, and who is goal oriented. All of us will agree that we are surrounded by people who do not have goals or projects that they are working on. In this way, they spend their time watching television, playing video games on their computers, and the biggest one of all, strolling on their social media sites and consuming everything that they see. It becomes a daily conversation, and you don't listen to the things that they're talking about, so you don't pay any attention to what they're saying. The reason for this is because you are striving to achieve your goals. You need to go out and find the right people to assist you in achieving the goals you have set for yourself. Otherwise, you may find yourself in a position that you do not wish to be in.

QUESTIONS

1. Define staying in focus.
   _____
   _____

2. Why are you not staying focus?
   _____
   _____

3. Which tasks should you prioritize? _____
   _____
   _____

4. What is the most important task to focus on first?_____
   _____
   _____

5. Why staying focus is the key to your success?
   _____
   _____

6. What are the benefits of being in focus? _____
   _____
   _____

7. How does being focus benefit your personal and professional life?

_____

_____

_____

8. What would you lose by not staying focus? _____

_____

_____

HOW TO STAY FOCUS

You have set a goal that you want to achieve and remain focused. Staying focused should be your number one priority. Having set a goal is the first step towards reaching that goal. The next step to be taken is to stay focused on your objectives.

In the absence of a goal, there is nothing to look forward to in the future. Let's take a moment to reflect on just how important it is to stay focused. It is impossible for you to accomplish any goal if you are not focused. Being the author of a book has been a challenge for me as I had to remain focus. The most productive time for me to focus on the day's work is early in the morning. I begin my day with a cup of coffee and then I meditate on what I have to do. My favorite way of writing my tasks is on my tablet which I take with me wherever I go. Because I have written it down, I can stay focused on what I am doing.

The fact that I have written it down helps me concentrate on what I have written. I find that it helps me to go back to my notes in order to stay focused on my tasks and to meditate on it. My personal blueprint to accomplish my task can be found in the form of writing it down. When I read it and put it into action, this is a sure way for me to complete the task. Training your mind to stay focused can be a very complicated responsibility. There are times when we all lose focus on what we are doing. Humanity has that tendency, so the idea is to train your mind to recognize when you are losing focus.

In order to achieve success and wealth, people need to focus on our goals and stay there. Regardless of what you are trying to accomplish, you need to stay focused to succeed. In order to remain wealthy, wealthy people focus on making more money and staying wealthy. A college student is focused on graduating from college. The point is that everyone who is trying to accomplish a goal has to stay focused. As far as I am concerned, there is no way around it.

The fact that things happen in life is a constant ~~fact of life~~. There will be certain things that are beyond your control and there will be nothing you can do about them. The one thing that really helped me stay focused was to eliminate negativity from my life and isolate myself from certain people. To stop associating with people who have negative energy, I cut off all contact with them. There are times when things happen outside of my control and that were beyond my control. However, as I take a step back, I analyze the situation and deal with it in accordance When I am in the middle of working on a job and an emergency arises, I have to think about it and put some changes into place so that I can accomplish the mission in both places while continuing to work on the job. There is no point in getting frustrated and angry if you don't want anything to change. I will not be able to change it by allowing it to stress me out. Staying focused and working through it helped me each time.

Life is full of situations, and we have to face the fact that not all situations can be ignored in life. The point I am trying to make here is that you shouldn't disregard family matters. Family is of course the most important thing in the world. The importance of staying focused on the goal, even if that means rearranging some things in the process. As we all deal with the mundane issues of daily life, we are all in the same boat.

There is no doubt that it is easy to lose focus when those mundane things of life happen to you. There is no doubt that it can get you off track at times. The loss of a spouse, the loss of a job, you or a loved one is experiencing health challenges are several things that can get you off track, and you need to allow yourself the time to deal with those issues and get back on track. As a result of losing your spouse and having to relocate, you may have a hard time staying focused on writing that manuscript. We all fall from time to time, and this is when we have to be determined to stand up again and go after our dreams.

No matter what I was facing, I had to stay focused because I had a family to provide for, and I had to do my best. It was my responsibility and they relied fully on me to do so. It was impossible for me to allow myself to be consumed for a long period of time in any situation in my life.

Let me share a short story with you.

In 2015, my mother passed away while I was working on a contract job. My customer understood and told me to go and take care of everything I needed to do, and then come back. In the week following my mother's funeral on that Saturday, I took an additional week off, and on Monday, I returned to work. To be able to complete my job and provide for my family, I had to remain focused throughout it all. I would like reiterate the point that things of life are bound to happen. Regardless of what life throws at you, it is imperative that you remain focused on your goal in order to achieve it.

As I mentioned above, the point I am trying to make here is that even though I lost my mother, I remained focused on my daily tasks and my goals throughout the process. The fact that I had employees working for me meant that payroll had to be processed. There were still bills to pay. You can rest assured that it is in no way an easy task. As difficult a challenge as this one might have been for me, it was probably one of the greatest challenges I have ever faced in my life so far.

In order to achieve your goal, I suggest the you use the five steps I have outlined: (1) mediate, (2) write down your goals, (3) study the written plan, (4) determine how you will achieve your goal, and (5) make a plan of action.

The first thing I do when I wake up in the morning is grab a hot cup of delicious coffee. I I head for my favorite chair on my front porch with my calendar book in hand to record my plans for today. This is. where. It all begins for me.

In this way, I can get things done in an orderly manner. Otherwise, I am prone to wander all over the place. The best way for me to be effective is to write it down. In an eight-hour day, I accomplish a lot of things. The way in which I plan to achieve that goal is a very important part of my strategy. Once again, this is my blueprint for success. There is a saying in my line of business: "Plan your work and let your plan guide your work."

There is no doubt that those five steps can make a big difference in achieving the goal that you have set for yourself. However, in order to see tangible results, we need to follow—not just read—these steps. As part of your daily routine, you should make sure to incorporate them into your mornings. In the end, if you follow these steps you will be able to reach your goal. How do I know that? This formula has worked very well for me every time I follow it.

The thing about writing things down is that they stay with you more than just thinking about them; I know this for a fact because I do it all the time. It was my mother who taught me how important it is to write things down. Throughout my childhood, I watched my mother write things down, and I learned from her how to do the same thing as well. She wrote down instructions and chores that had to be done. It was important for her to make a grocery list and write down when the bills needed to be paid. She demonstrated this important habit time and time again.

The more you try to remember everything, the more it will slip your mind. Using these five steps has helped me accomplish goals and I know that it will help you to accomplish yours as well.

Let's identify whether you're in focus or out of focus and what distractions you are experiencing. This is where you take a long look at the person in the mirror. What is the best way for you to stay focused?

Throughout the process of writing this book, I have found it easier to stay focused by writing down my goals and using it as a guide or blueprint for the day.

No matter what you want to accomplish, you need a guideline or a blueprint. This book is designed to be a blueprint that can help you no matter what your goals are. Try these five steps and you will be happy with the end results. Remember, you have to put the work and time in.

Let me give you a personal example. It's my wish to retire at some point, so I established a goal to set aside X amount of dollars in my 401K plan believing my financial situation will be stable when the day arrives. In order to achieve this, I am required to stay focused on investing in my 401K. The first thing I had to do was to make sure I did not withdraw funds from my 401K. If I did withdraw money, then I had to make sure I paid it back to avoid paying a penalty and I had to deposit the additional target amount as I had promised myself I would do. For this retirement goal to be reached, I have to stay focused.

In the last two years, COVID has had an impact on millions of people. Thousands of people have lost their focus due to the pandemic. There is no doubt that some people's attention span has been reduced to the bare minimum. Due to one natural disaster after another, they have lost focus, concentration, and even their motivation.

There is a lack of focus. There is no doubt that this chapter is of utmost importance. In this chapter, you will learn how to come back into focus and how to keep your focus so that you can achieve your goal. There are numerous examples of people neglecting themselves, not going to school, overeating and drinking, and other unwanted habits. You can say they are "out of focus" if you want to be more precise.

It is important that you gather your thoughts and learn how to write them down with as much detail as possible. It is recommended that you read it aloud every day. You should make sure to wake up and go to bed at the same time each day. Developing good habits can help you become a successful person. It will not help you achieve that goal if you spend all day sleeping, staying up all night watching television, watching videos, playing games, or scrolling through social media sites. You have to be disciplined if you want to succeed. The five steps will help you get on track for the first time and get back on track when things get out of focus.

Are you wandering or lost?

You can get lost and ask somebody for directions and get back in line. In Joshua 5-6, the children of Israel wandered for forty years. Because they disobeyed God. They disobeyed God's word and they built false gods. In other words, if you disobey the blueprint of your life, you will be like the children of Israel, you will constantly wander.

Yoga is like a form of meditation, where you block out everything and give your body, your mind, and your soul attention as needed. It is called "you time". Time for you to go within yourself and be honest with yourself. Again, meditation takes time. You just can't do it just by saying, "I want to do it." You have to put forth the effort, you just can get back on focus. It takes some time and you have to apply intentional, focused effort not be haphazard.

There is a goal that you want to accomplish if you are reading this book, otherwise, you wouldn't be reading this book. In other words, your mind is made and are set to accomplish your goal or task. A mind-over-matter approach is what it takes to succeed. To put it simply, it comes down to the fact that your mind needs to be trained. You will be able to accomplish all the tasks on your list and successfully follow your blueprint once you learn how to train your mind. It will put you closer to the finish line as you begin to accomplish task after tasks. And as much as possible, minimize distractions.

We are going to use this book as a tool to help you understand the issues you have that are causing you to lose focus. You will be able to see where you are in your life through this book. There is no doubt in my mind that you will know exactly where you are. The goal is to see yourself clearly and become enlightened. It has been written with the purpose of helping you identify both your shortfalls and your strengths to help you improve your performance.

Write you goals and post it on the refrigerator, in your car, on the wall, write it down on a sticky note, and stick it on the mirror so that you see it every morning while you are taking care of your hygiene. It doesn't matter what it is, just do it. If you want to talk about it a few times. Sometimes, there may not be anyone around to talk to, so you have to talk it out with yourself. This is something I do quite often. Matter of fact, it better sometimes not to discuss your plans with others. Sometimes other people can discourage and distract you from accomplishing that goal or task. Therefore, I have no problems keeping my plan of action to myself. It has worked for me over and over again.

QUESTIONS

1. What is focus?_____
_____

2. How can you stay in focus? _____
_____
_____
_____

3. Do you lose focus easily?_____

4. Can you get back on focus easily?_____

5. What can you do to get back in focus?
   _____
_____
_____

6. How can you prioritize your focus? _____
_____
_____

7. Why do you think it's so important to stay in focus? _____
_____
_____

8. What does it cost to get or stay out of focus?_____

PROTECTING YOUR FOCUS

Having your goals set and making sure that they are accomplished is what it is all about. To do that, you have to remain focused and you have to protect your ~~focus to do that~~. You may get sidetracked by something. It may take you longer than you had anticipated. As a result of protecting your focus, you are learning how to stay on track. I mentioned earlier that it does not matter whether it is an emergency or not since an emergency will happen at some point anyway. It is still necessary to come back to it and focus on what you need to do.

There was something that happened that particular day in your life and it affected you in some way. All other things, however, continue to go on as normal. You can be detained, but you cannot stop what you are doing. It is possible to detain you for a minute, but you cannot stop. Even though this emergency came up, it is important to understand. My focus is shifting back and I'm trying to get back on track. As soon as you recognize that you are. When you recognize that you are out of focus, you need to get back focus as quickly as possible.

Are you allowing the distractions to keep you from doing what you should be doing? The truth is, it is judicious to maximize your focus enough so that you can recognize when you're off track. This is because you need to stop and take care of yourself. When you are in focus, you know exactly when you need to take action.

In truth, you won't be able to achieve your goals if you don't. To a certain extent, you're not selfish by doing it, but it's something you have to do. It is impossible to respond to everything that comes your way. It is impossible for you to attend every function. It drains you and takes entirely too much energy for you to stay focused.

It is important to understand your limitations. There are times I must step back and evaluate myself and learn to delegate if need be. We sometimes allow ourselves to be consumed with other people's issues even when it doesn't involve us. This is truly something that you want to avoid.

It is important that you keep your focus on what is important at all times. There is no doubt that I am spending too much time here. As a result, I need to do things to ensure everything is taken care of for everyone else as well. I gotta look out for number one. And that's what has to be done.

In other words, your physical, as well as your mental well-being, are intertwined, and you need to protect both. Like Reese's Peanut Butter Cups, you can't have one without the other. So, therefore, we must take care of ourselves and set aside time for ourselves as well in order to maintain and stay in focus.

It is for this reason that a person needs to be able to identify what is intruding on their focus. Occasionally, people will enter your space to distract you. I think it is important that you learn how to protect that space at all times in your life. In some cases, you must cut off some people or give yourself time away from them for a period of time. You might be spending a lot of time on social media and watching too much television, and I believe that your cell phone can be a distraction as well. It is possible to spend too much time watching too much news, too much negativity, and this will lead to a lot of distractions. There is no doubt that you are losing focus and you are not protecting your focus at all.

We should all work on protecting our focus so that we can do what we do with excellence. As I said earlier, let me be clear here, this is something that all of us should learn to master if we want to achieve our goals. Are people aware of the importance of protecting their focus regularly? As a general rule, most people do not think about protecting their focus, and therefore they will have a hard time accomplishing any goal.

Our focus can be thrown off by the mundane things of life from time to time. A person who is serious about achieving their goal will have no trouble getting back on track if they are committed to it. There is no doubt that they are aware of the fact that they must protect their concentration at all costs if they are to accomplish their task. Do you consider yourself to be someone of that kind? If that is not the case, would you like to be a person like that?

Keeping my focus is one of the most important things I do. I tell my wife often that if it does not have anything to do with me, I am not interested in discussing it. I politely made it clear to her that I would rather not discuss that topic. The point I am trying to make here is that it is not my business or my affairs, it is someone else's. I am, therefore, not interested in engaging in such a type of conversation. By taking that action, I have once again been able to protect my focus.

Let's take a moment to look closer at it.

Quite a few of the people who she may be referring to, I am not familiar with. Consequently, I am not interested in engaging in a conversation about other people's business affairs or personal affairs that I am not familiar with. As far as I am concerned, that is a complete waste of time. Protecting my time and focusing on what is important to me and my family is a priority for me.

The purpose of this chapter is to teach you how to protect your focus. The only person who can accomplish this is you. Once you have practiced it for a while, it will become second nature to you after a short period. It doesn't matter what is taking place around you. Having learned how important it is to protect our focus to achieve our goals in the future, you will scale back and prevent most unnecessary distractions.

Some people must be cut off. The phone must be turned off. Radios, televisions, social media, and email or text notifications must be turned off. They are distracting you from your goal. The decision is yours to make. Focus is a precious thing, and it must be protected at all costs. It is imperative that you take care of yourself because if you don't, you will fall ill and you won't be able to help anybody else. Therefore, we must know our limitations.

I would like to share with you a scripture that I read. In the first chapter in the book of Joshua, God tells Joshua that Moses is dead. "Nevertheless, as I was with Moses, I will also be with you."

It is because of this scripture that I am confident that God takes care of me. Having said that, I know that if I stay focused and do what I must, then He will take care of the outcome. In other words, I do what I'm supposed to do. I have a scripture that I read every day, and I sit with the meditation daily, because it helps me in my consistent walk. This scripture is the foundation for my success and strength. Psalm 51: I have Mercy on according to thy love and kindness.

There are more distractions now than ever before. So, protecting our focus is more important now. The reason we need to point out these distractions is because we didn't have them twenty-five years ago, and now that we have them, we have to intentionally recognize and remove them. There is too much going on around us and we fall off track because of this. There is no doubt that the state of your mind is the most important thing in your life. How do you protect your focus so that what is important to you stays in maximum focus? Are you conscious of it every single day of your life? Is it something you think about?

My walk with Christ is an ongoing part of my daily living, and I am aware of it every single moment. I am a regular attendee of Midweek Bible Study and Sunday church services, Over the last sixty plus years, I have dedicated myself to learning and living the Word of God. In no way am I claiming to be perfect. It is important to remember that the Word is what I use to get back on track when I fall off track. There is no doubt about it: I am insured by the Word of God. There is a certain sense of security in knowing that the goals I have set can be achieved by my personal and relationship with Christ. I personally can say it is the best insurance for me. God's instructions are very helpful in my walk and with the challenges that I have to deal with daily. It is through His words that I find strength and I make every effort to protect my belief at all costs. Having said that, what happens if you don't protect your beliefs about staying focus? In the end, there is a possibility of a bad outcome. As time goes on, we find that things do not go as planned because we are not focused on what we are doing. In other words, we are subject to the same fate.

As I was reflecting on this, I was reminded of some of the successful entertainers and celebrities, like the famous Jackson family. The father, Joe Jackson, made sure that his children put in hours upon hours of practice in order to succeed. In the end, it paid off for them. However, they had to make significant sacrifices along the way. The children were not allowed to go outside or play with their friends outside of school. They had to practice singing and dancing as much as they could. Now, look at them today. Obviously, there will be some sacrifices to be made on your part. Do you know what those sacrifices are? Focus is the key to achieving whatever goal you have in mind. There are times when you get setbacks, there is nothing wrong with a setback when you realize it, and you know that you have to overcome it to get to where you want to go. In other words, don't let sacrifices make you lose sight of what you're trying to achieve. Keep your focus, and don't forget that any setback can distract you from your goals.

When you do not protect your focus, you're setting yourself up for failure. Regarding the question about being selfish with your time, I can tell you first of all that it is not being selfish at all. Rather, it is being focused on what you want to accomplish. Therefore, I would advise you to go ahead and be selfish here. That's what you're doing, you're staying focused on your goals, and that's a very important thing to do to achieve what you want.

There is no point in worrying about your weaknesses. The key is to recognize them and to start improving as soon as possible. That's exactly what the key is!

Ultimately, only you can decide when and how to focus and only you can change it. The purpose of this book is to serve as a guide to help you accomplish what you want to achieve. Focus is one of the most important things that must be protected, and there is no doubt about that. As a result, you need to get organized in writing down your goals and plan of action. As you see, this advice is repeated in almost every chapter of the book. If it wasn't so important, I wouldn't repeat the same advice over and over again. Write it down. Identify what you are trying to achieve, describe how you will become successful at getting there, and explain how you will stay focused. The rest of the things will work out just fine. At the end of the day, the results will be beautiful. Yes, that's right. There is no doubt in our minds that we are in good hands.

We've had significant achievements, and we are sure that everything we have done has been for the best. Rest assured that the outcome will be good we understand the balance of the focus. It is because of your focus that you will be able to receive a benefit in the future.

There is no doubt about it. You may have to spend some time on this and make sacrifices. It is going to cost you some effort. It is going to cost you some friends. It will come with some negativity, and it will cost you some family time. However, in order to be successful, you have to remain focused. This is imperative. Staying focused and protecting your focus are two of the most important things you must not lose sight of.

QUESTIONS

1. Why should you protect your focus?_____
   _____
   _____

2. What are you protecting?_____
   _____
   _____

3. Why should you protect your focus?_____
   _____
   _____

4. What are the benefits to protecting your focus? _____
   _____
   _____

5. What are the end results if you do not protect your focus? ___
   _____
   _____

6. Who is responsible for protecting your focus?_____
   _____

7. What will it take for you to succeed? Are you willing to do what it takes? _____
   _____

THE POWER OF CONCENTRATION

You can lose focus in the blink of an eye. Earlier, we discussed the mundane things in life that can make you stop concentrating and begin to lose focus if you don't watch out for them. As a result, you need to learn and practice how to not allow life's mundane things to distract you from accomplishing the task or goal you have set out to achieve.

You must stay focused throughout the process. For you to be able to achieve what you are trying to accomplish, you must practice every day. The right perspective is the key to success. There is no doubt that all of your goals are important, but prioritizing them is the critical for staying on track. Try to make it a habit not to be engaged in anything other than what you are doing. Minimize the attention you pay to things that don't concern you, your family, or the task at hand. This is another added dimension that sidetracked you from your original goal. Whenever you start doing or worrying about things that have nothing to do with you, it will take you off track and completely pull you away from what you need to do.

There is something you would like to change or you wouldn't be reading this book. It's going to be necessary for you to eliminate some things from your life and focus on the goals you want to achieve in your life. Life is full of distractions that you encounter as you go about your daily activities. It is necessary for you to avoid them in order to succeed in life. At the end of this chapter, you will be able to write down the things that hinder your ability to concentrate.

Make sure you stay focused on your goal at all times. It is a good idea to write the goals down every day or before you go to bed. It is recommended that you write it down and read it out loud a couple of times a day. Keep track of your goals and create your own blueprint to live by it. Remember, concentration is the key to achieving all of your goals.

When I was a child, I remember going to Sunday School and hearing the Sunday School teacher tell the class that no matter what happens "God is in control." Even though bad things happened in my life, I know that God is in control, and something good is going to come from it in the end. Because of this, you just have to stay focused and keep doing what you do. Tell yourself, "As long as I keep in mind that everything will be all right in the end. I know that I can concentrate better and reach my goals!"

It is important to have a clear understanding of what you are trying to accomplish. It's important—as I've mentioned many times throughout this book—that you stay focused, concentrate on what you're doing, and block out everything that takes you away from your work. It is essential for everyone to have their own space where they can think, meditate, and concentrate.

For you to accomplish your goals, there may be many things that you will need to give up for the moment for you to achieve them. You may go out to the pool party, have a night out with my friends, or go shopping with my friends, but the only person who can tell you what you have to give up is you. You already know the things that consistently distract you. It is your choice and the consequences are yours when you do not stay focused and concentrate.

You have to choose what you want to achieve. For you to achieve your goals, you need to spend as much time as you can alone. You need to put in a lot of hard work, to burn the midnight oil, stay away from distractions, and isolate or remove people who are hindering your success and growth in your life. It is a process and you must comprehend that concentration is a very. Important part of focus. It is essential that both go in sequence for it to be effective.

The following are the steps that need to be taken.

Make a promise to yourself. The importance of taking an oath to yourself cannot be overstated. There would be no point in reading this book and using a guide if you didn't need it. Obviously, you know what needs to be done and what you need to do to maintain that success.

Don't forget. Keep it in your memory. When you do that, you commit yourself to your purpose and to your goal. I believe that it is so important to write down your goals and read them aloud.

Work on developing a plan of action and implementing it as soon as possible. You should cultivate your mind first before anything else. Consequently, it will help you achieve and maintain your goals. Let's be honest, everyone has something they want to accomplish, but the question is, how do they accomplish it? It is important to ask yourself, "How can you accomplish your goal?" By answering the questions at the end of this chapter, you will gain a better understanding of what you have to do in order to accomplish your goal.

Focus on what you have read and then act on it. If you don't take action now, you may regret it later on in life.

Today, people have so many distractions that prevent them from concentrating. During the early morning, I meditate and concentrate on the things I need to accomplish for the day. My daily schedule and tasks are written on a Things-to-Do list beside my bed. For example, if I need to order supplies and materials for a job. If I don't write it down, I'll forget and that will affect my entire workday. My point is that if I don't write it down, it will have a bad outcome. Make a note of it!

Practice and change things that are hindering your growth in order to concentrate well. Change old habits and develop new ones. Replace bad habits with good ones. We all have bad habits that need broken. Bad habit can be a hinderance and a major distraction.

If you want to concentrate, you need to set aside time for it. Everything has its season, everything has its time. Practice concentrating on what you must do to achieve your goals.

If you want to achieve what you want, you will need to change each and every hindering habit. You are fully responsible for this. The only person responsible for your lack of achievement is you. Not anyone else. The best thing you can do is to be true to yourself. You are the subject of the book. The goal is to help you achieve your goals and evolve as a person, whether it is becoming a better student, starting a business, applying for a grant, or becoming a better parent.

If you are being honest with yourself, write down the good, the bad, and the ugly. Our emotions, our behavior, and our finances can cause us to spend a lot of time and money on things that are just a waste of time and money. Every aspect of our lives can benefit from being in focus.

Therefore, it is for this very reason that you are taking the initiative to bring to the fore what you aren't doing. There are many benefits to this book as a result of the information it contains. Concentration is one of the most important aspects of life that cannot be overstated.

By not meditating, you are not providing yourself with a quiet place to contemplate your life or your goals. Concentration is the key to achieving your goal. You are the one who is implementing it.

When you are working, concentrating on what you are doing, and staying focused you will be able to accomplish what you set your mind to. A person concentrates when they have a particular goal in mind, and then they focus on acting on that goal or completing that particular task.

You need to make concentrating and meditating a part of your daily routine. It is important to practice every day. Can you tell me about some of the rewards you received as a result of your efforts? Are you going to be able to remain focused? When you concentrate and when you meditate do you think about your goals? What were some of the goals that you were able to accomplish during the year?

It may be a financial goal that you are trying to achieve, but you have to minimize unnecessary spending in order to achieve your goal. It is important to understand what you are trying to achieve, as well as why it is important to you. The second thing that you need to ask yourself is, what are you willing to give up in order to achieve this goal? Is it possible for you to stop shopping, going out to eat on a weekly basis, and spending access money if you want to do that?

The advantage of concentration is that it makes what you are doing come out in a positive way as the outcome of what you are doing comes out in a positive way as well. Concentration has several benefits that can be attributed to it. In a nutshell, that is what it is all about. There is going to be a release at some point. If you aren't concentrating on what you want to achieve, you won't achieve it. This could lead to a lot of bad things happening in the future.

For example, it is unsafe for me to be distracted in my work as an electrician. I have to concentrate on my line of work. If I am not focused on it, there is a good chance that I could get hurt, killed, or electrocuted. Yes, that's correct. Even though the phone is ringing at a high pitch, you blocked it out because I'm doing something else.

Like me, you must keep focus on what you are doing and concentrate only on that is very significant.

It is imperative that we practice regardless of what the situation may be. The purpose of this book is to change some of the practices that are currently in place. Change our thought patterns and change our way of doing things.

To stay focused on what needs to be done. The essence of enlightenment involves bringing understanding to what you are doing, or not doing.

In order for me to succeed in this task, I must remain focused and concentrate. Keeping that in mind, in order to keep going as plan, I had to reflect my schedule and task that record during my prayer and mediation time. I had to do a lot of concentration in some aspects of my personal life because I got of focus. which had a negative effect on my performance. So, as a result, I had to get back on track with my life and get a bad track focus on it. This would lead to the outcome. I believe the outcome will be positive.

When I was in the first grade, I found that sometimes it was difficult to concentrate and that my teacher did not hesitate to punish me if I did not pay attention and concentrate on the subject she was teaching. Let's not be surprised when life punishes us for not paying attention when we know that we should.

Stay focused. The importance of concentration cannot be overstated. By now you've written the things that you need to concentrate on, so go back and read it. Take a moment now and focus on what you've written. We are all affected when we are not concentrating or when we have lost focus. Once you get off track, it is difficult to get back on track. It's definitely not impossible, but it's not easy either.

What happens to you when you do not concentrate and meditate? Once you decide where you're falling short, you act it out and that makes you better at what you're doing.

Again, it all starts with you. I think that's what we are aiming to achieve from that, and that's what the goal is. We have to set a goal within ourselves so that we can have something to look forward to in the future so that we can have something to look forward to. Once you've set your goal, stay focused and keep working.

It is common for people to say that they do not have the ability to concentrate. This happened to me and I got distracted by it. That sounds so mundane to me. Is that all there is to it?

Yes, that's correct. There are a few things we have to leave out, and we have to do that. This is how we are able to get back on track and get these things out of the way. That's when we all focus on staying focused, that's when we can all stay focused. How can you minimize some of the distractions from your life so that you can meditate and focus on things that are going to bring us the greatest success in your life?

By following the formulas that have been given to you, you will be able to achieve the goals you have set for yourself. Stay focused and get to work.

QUESTIONS

1. Do you have a difficult time concentrating? _____

_____

_____

2. What do you think is the problem with you concentrating? _____

_____

_____

3. What do you think you need to do start concentrating? _____

_____

_____

4. When is the best time for you to concentrate and mediate? _____

_____

5. What are you concentrating on at this moment? _____

_____

_____

_____

6. How does writing things down help you focus? _____

_____

_____

7. Why is concentration important? _____

THE POWER OF PRAYERS AND MEDITATION

Let's talk about the power of focus through meditation and prayers. There is a relationship between words, meditations, prayers, and focus. Throughout this book, I've shared the relationship between the words, mediations, prayers, and focus. Well, they go hand-in-hand. Whenever you meditate, you train your thoughts to go deeply into a safe place inside of you that only you can enter. It doesn't matter if that time of medication is in the morning, midday, afternoon, or night. You need to find the time daily to meditate.

I find that mornings work perfectly for me. When the morning is fresh, the sun is rising and the quietness of the morning is there, I can hear my thoughts clearer. It's just me and God. It's just me and myself. Before I get too busy with my daily chores and those mundane things of life happens, go to that place where you can meditate on your tasks and goals. You have a full day ahead. To plan how you're going to go about your day, you need to meditate, pray, and focus.

Surely, you can separate yourself for a few minutes out of the day to pray and meditate to receive a guide or method to follow. I found that my best time to meditate is in the mornings before I prepare to attend church, go to work, or go to class. Make it your practice immediately. Before you prepare breakfast, drink coffee, or whatever, go into your secret closet, where you can be by yourself and commune with God and yourself in a spiritual prayer or meditation. It's a method that fully relaxes me. It helps me focus and learn to block out everything that's on my mind while aiding me to focus on a greater connection with God. This is a proven method that has helped many people.

So, therefore, just practice and practice some more. By doing this, you put yourself in a state that is almost automatically set to keep you focused.

Instead of working on everyone else's projects, it is time to work on your own purpose, goals, and mission. Sometimes we will put others' projects and missions before our own. Remember it's okay to say "no".

You have to look out for yourself to set time aside and maintain focus. Get away from everything and everybody and block out distractions.

Now, I know it's hard for a mother with two children, a husband, and a home to work on developing her product. In situations, a mother will put her children's needs and wants before her own. However, the mother needs to sit with her husband and develop a plan that can help her accomplish her goals. A solution may be to have daily meals planned, or to hire someone to help with chores, or for dad to take the kids to the park every Saturday and give his wife time to work on her purpose or passions. What she can accomplish in a few hours will make all the difference.

In today's world, we're so busy which is more of a reason why we need to plan our days out. We are all given the same twenty-four hours to a day. Now, how you spend time is up to you. How you plan it is up to you. Make time for yourself in that twenty-four hours. If you believe you can't find twenty minutes to work on your goals and your dreams, you're only fooling yourself. If you study the life of millionaires, one thing you will find with each and every last one of them is they are driven by many forces of accomplishment. They want to expand the business, invest in more stock, and develop the community. They know that time is money and they do not have to waste it. They don't have time to waste on conversations or activities that will not be fruitful.

I know I wanted to finish writing my book, and that meant weekly meetings and consistent writing. I was conscious of the time, and I watched the clock because I didn't want to overextend myself on the job and not be able to work later on this book. I wanted to achieve a certain goal when I was on the job site so I could work with my editor knowing confidently that I'd accomplished my goal for the day. I realized that her time was valuable and I didn't want to cause a chain reaction for my delay if I were to reschedule, so I made a commitment to her and to me.

Let's go back to meditation. Let's talk about your own experience with meditation. How deep have you gotten in meditation? And what was your experience like? Because meditation doesn't come easy. That's right. You have to work at this. Write down your goals and visions. Then write down how you plan to achieve this goal. You have to put forward the action, time, and effort to make it happen. In the morning, when you wake up, pray and meditate before you get your day started.

> *Seek first the Kingdom of Heaven, and all things will be added to you.*
>
> *Matthew 6:33*

Each of us can go in and out of focus at times. There are times when things don't go as planned. Our focus shifts from praying and meditating to other things. Prayer is a communion with God, and we should meditate constantly, every day, and make it a part of our lives. We are in communion with a higher power when we pray. Giving thanks and asking for guidance is another important part of prayer.

Sometimes you can't share your vision, dreams, or goals with people who don't share their own. Your vision wasn't given to them. Some people can live their entire lives without meditating, never knowing what meditation can do. Don't let the mundane things of life keep you from praying and meditating. My success and my life are built on this foundation.

Making time for yourself is the point I'm trying to make here. Although you may have other responsibilities, you need ten to twenty minutes before you start your morning or before you go to sleep. It is up to you to pray and meditate, you have to do it on your own. You have to think deeper, focusing on one thought for a while to accomplish this. It is up to you as an individual to make it happen. Regardless of how busy your schedule may become, find the time for prayer and meditation. By doing so, you are on the right track to achieving your goals, missions, and purposes.

If you have an hour lunch break, take ten minutes to meditate and pray, put your cell phone down, get away from your colleagues, and just find a quiet place. It will refresh you and help you get through the remainder of the date with clarity. Meditation helps you stay focused and it helps you not to let your mind wander. By blocking everything out, you keep your mind from wandering. Meditation is also beneficial to your spiritual journey. My point is just that you need to make it happen.

You can use this to help you with stress and other issues that may hinder your success. Everyone gets distracted and has to get back on track. Getting off track is easy, and getting back on track can be challenging. You have to block out other things if you want to achieve something and you know what it will take. Sometimes we can meditate on what we want to accomplish. Throughout the day, we think about it. There is no doubt that you have it on your mind. In fact, you are probably always thinking about it. There is a form of meditation that goes along with that. As I am going through the day, which I have already meditated this morning and have been focusing on what I am going to do, now is coming up in my mind as

I go through the day. My goal is to complete my task and goal as soon as possible, so I am going to make it happen. The way I stay focused, the way I pray, the way I stay in communion with God, that's how I stay in focus. I consider this to be one of the most important parts of my life's blueprint: to continually seek and maintain a closer relationship with God in order to be able to serve Him better.

The Bible contains many references to meditation. In fact, the Bible mentions meditation twenty-three times. In the book of Psalms alone, the word meditation is mentioned nineteen times. Why would it be mentioned so often if it were not necessary? Reading these scriptures helps me stay focused.

Distractions keep us from God, and He wants us to get away from them. You need to get away from those things that can separate you and Him. This is why it is so important for us to meditate on a daily basis.

How you evolve is largely influenced by your surroundings. You can sometimes be negatively affected by the environment around you. It is important to keep yourself away from negativity. Whether it's negativity from a family member, coworker, or church member, you need to cut them off. Make sure you create a space that makes you comfortable so you can meditate effectively. It encompasses the mind, the body, and the soul.

Keeping calm, practicing breathing techniques, creating a special time of the day, and learning to relax after a busy day are essential. It's your time, your time to spend in prayer and meditation with God. It's just you and Him all by yourself. If you take the time to set aside time just for Him, as you meditate and pray, you will see greater results.

The best way to prepare yourself for your day is to meditate before you begin it. The fact is that meditation can indeed help you deal with anything that might come your way on that particular day, no matter what it is. Suppose, for example, that you are driving to work and you hear people blowing horns, you won't let them distract you from driving. There may be reasons that you are not aware of that could temporarily hinder your progress because unforeseen events will occur at some point in time. It is best to let the process run its course.

Whatever you want to accomplish in life depends on you having the disciple to spend those ten or twenty minutes (or however long you set aside) to reflect and plan. You need to concentrate on that one thought and talk to God for as long as it takes, not on how long it takes in minutes.

Plan how you will start the day. In some cases, you know what's going to happen, and you can prepare. Meditation and prayer are therefore important. When you release power, you are able to accomplish your goals or overcome adversity. By coping and handling any circumstance that directly affects you, you learn how to handle any situation.

Making time and setting our daily goals is very important. Each of us needs a book that teaches us to stay focused. To make time, you need to create, you need to be proactive, and you need to make it happen. It is for this reason that prayer and meditation are so important.

Remember, this book is designed to enlighten you on what you are and are not doing. Are you praying and meditating? Are you writing down your goal for the day and planning your activities? Have you noticed what consistently distracts you? Have you considered ways to minimize those distractions and maximize your focus? Praying and meditating must be part of your daily routine if you haven't done so already. To stay focused and meet your goal, you will need to change the way you do a few things. Setting aside time for meditation helps us to understand that God will provide everything we need to accomplish our goals. God gives us the opportunity to communicate with him.

Keeping focused on what we're going to do, and what project we're working on, keeps us focused and assures us that everything will work out. By not allowing the mundane to distract us, we are growing in our meditation and faith. We are in good hands because God promises never to leave us nor forsake us.

That's also what helps me when I meditate, knowing that He will do it because He promised me He would. According to His scriptures, He will take care of everything. The Hebrew 13:5 verse. In the Bible, it is mentioned 25 times to reassure us that he will always be there for us.

Despite not having to meditate in a quiet place, I value meditation. However, a quiet place is helpful. The time of day does not matter to me when I meditate. Since I've been doing it for so long, it's become second nature to me. Initially, it wasn't easy for me. Throughout the years, I have learned to master it and am still working on it.

Find a method or system that is right for you. Instead of wandering, we should get back to following the scriptures and obeying God's plans. We will need to restructure our system to remain focused and communicate effectively in the future. It is necessary to have a blueprint when building a house. Having a blueprint is the best way to ensure that you will be able to accomplish your goal. Whatever the case may be, there is no difference between the two. For me to fulfill my dream of becoming a published author, I had to find the right people who could assist me in writing my book and follow the process. Yes, I have the words to express myself. What about a book editor, cover designer, and someone to help me format it? To achieve that goal, I set out to find the right people.

When it comes to my goals and dreams, I learned not to share them with people who cannot help me or who try to discourage me from achieving them. Surrounding yourself with the right people is imperative. It's part of your goal. God will answer your prayers if you ask Him for help finding the right people. While I was on the job site, I thought I was doing an electrical job, not knowing that I was going to meet the person who would help me publish this book.

You have to make time for meditation in order to be led right to where you need to be and with the people you need to be with. Everybody who looks over their day can find some wasted time. You will have to rearrange your schedule. I promise you., when we reevaluate our day, we will find that we are wasting valuable time somewhere. Just think about what you could have accomplished with the time wasted.

My day begins with prayer and meditation. It works for me, and I hope it will work for you as well. You have nothing to lose by praying and meditating, but you have everything to gain. You may be interested in starting a business, becoming a doctor or attorney, or just trying to get out of debt or lose weight. It can be as simple as trying to become a better person. It doesn't matter what your goal is, prayer and meditation are crucial. It shouldn't hurt to try, after all, you have already tried everything. Don't be afraid to try and see what happens.

What's holding you back? You have what it takes, so, what's holding you back? What are the benefits of allow it to keep you stuck? You are the only one who can determine that. Don't forget to stay true to yourself. We can all blame our failures on anyone and everything. In the end, we know the truth.

Set an alarm or a reminder for you to pray. To achieve our goals in life, and to stay focused, we must practice this every day. You'll look forward to that time of prayer and meditation. Your daily routine becomes accustomed to it after a while.

Are you of the opinion that people should meditate no matter what is going on around them? Things will happen, I'm not saying they won't. Consider, for instance, the death of a family member. It doesn't mean that you shouldn't meditate or work on your goals. Having lost family members myself, I know how difficult it is. Let me assure you, I still had to pay my bills, pick up my children from school, and go to work. Despite the loss of family, life must still go on.

Life is full of other mundane things. Regardless of what's going on, we have to make time to accomplish our goals. In reading this book and answering the questionnaire about yourself, I'm trying to help you gain a better understanding of your shortcomings and create a personal strategy to staying in focus.

The key to finding out who you are is to get to know yourself -By practicing meditation, you will be able to see yourself and learn more about yourself. If we wish to become a better person, we must look in the mirror in order to see who we are. Reading this book is your first action to see the person you really are. There is no doubt that you want to become a better person, accomplish a goal, or accomplish a mission in life.

Growing up, I attended church in a small town called Independence, Louisiana. Mama used to take us to church on Sundays. Honestly, we didn't have much choice. Our household was built on this foundation. Mama warned us to pay attention. She'd better not turn around and see you goofing off.

Throughout my life, I have learned to pay attention to details. My life was shaped by it. It is possible to attribute many of my achievements to the lessons I learned in my early years. Mama, who was born in 1921, knew from her life's experiences that she had to pay attention. In her day, children grew up fast because they had so many responsibilities to help the family. I lost my father and the breadwinner of the house when I was only six years old. My mother became the head of the household and sole provider of eight children although we all had responsibilities. No matter what it took, Mama made sure the family prayed together. Prayers and meditation had a powerful effect on Mama. It worked for her, so it would work for her children and their children.

QUESTIONS

1. Do you believe in the power of prayers and meditation? _____

_____

_____

2. Have you spent time meditating? _____

_____

_____

3. When is the best time of the day for you to meditate? _____

_____

_____

4. How much time do you spend meditating? _____

_____

5. How can prayers and meditation can help you? _____

_____

_____

6. Why is prayers and meditation important? _____

_____

_____

7. How important is it to achieving your goal? _____

_____

_____

8. Would you make it a part of your daily routine? _____

_____

_____

GENERATIONAL FOCUS

The purpose of this chapter is to explore our family history and dynamics. Everyone's family is unique and has its own set of strengths as well as its own set of shortcomings. Are there any families that you are aware of that have been in the business for generations? Do you know a family of doctors, lawyers, educators, and other professionals? Does your family have a history of procrastinating? Is your family a party-going one? Is there such a thing as generational curses within your lineage? How do they work? Would you say that generational curses are a hindrance to your success?

We can all agree that there is something in all of our families that needs to be improved. Unfortunately, we live in a society that is plagued by dysfunction. The result of this can sometimes be the development of bad habits. It is not uncommon for our community to hear about things happening to families. Taking a child whose parents are on drugs as an example, a child who is in early grade school is unable to focus because of what is going on at home as a result of their parents' drug use. As a child, he grew up watching his father use drugs and drink excessively. The lifestyle of his grandfather and uncle is similar to that of his father. Three generations have been counted and each one lives in a similar way. If the child does not leave the environment, what are the most likely consequences?

In contrast, I saw my father provide for his family in another way. In my childhood, I recall my father bringing flowers to my mother on special occasions. It was in those days that I was a little boy who sat with my father in his black Impala Chevrolet watching him drive up and hand her the bouquet of flowers he had bought for her.

The smile on her face said everything about what she was feeling. The care my father gave to my mother was excellent. It was an expression of his love for her, as he showed kindness and gentleness to her and provided for their children as a way to express his love for her. I would say that my father spent most of his time at home as a farmer. His standards as a preacher, a man, and a father shaped me into the man I am today because of his standards and example.

In the course of becoming a man, I became a husband and father of a son and a daughter. I taught my children the same lessons that I had learned from my parents. My father and mother taught me the importance of good ethnicity by making sure I went to church on Sundays, instilling in them a sense of pride in their roots, just as they brought me up. I am proud of my children and the accomplishments they have made in their lives. In the previous paragraphs, we discussed the difference between a bad home environment and a good home environment.

As a child grows up, the environment in which he or she lives does not mean that the course of his or her life cannot change. There is a possibility of breaking generational curses if you are determined enough. When a child lives in a toxic environment, he or she can still be a straight-A student if they apply themselves and desire to do better. I had a childhood friend who lived in the woods with his family. The situation they were in was what you might call "dirt poor". For generations, they have lived in this manner. He was the first of his siblings and the first in his family to attend college. As a result of his efforts and focus, he has become a very successful man. He broke a generational curse.

The first step in breaking family curses in your family is to establish what you want to break. You may be wondering what you can do to change a family habit that is preventing you from reaching your goals. I sat down with the editor and we discussed different situations in my family that could be viewed as generational curses. One situation came up around family members with gambling addictions. Suppose you have a sibling who always asks you for money because of his or her gambling addiction. There has yet to be a repayment of the first loan. Another request has been made by them for a new one. By lending them the first money, you cut into an area that was very important to you and now you are unable to purchase a college textbook for your child. Even though you are not taking them to gamble or even encouraging their addiction, you are in a state of enablement.

Why is that so?

The reason for this is that you allow their bad habit to affect you and your family. At this point, you have to draw a line in the sand, otherwise, you would be working to support their gambling habit and continuing the curse. There has to be a limit to this and it may cause tension in the relationship, but you have to draw the line for yourself and your family in order to live a fulfilling life.

Generational focus and generational structure work together to provide a better understanding of generational wealth. Let me tell you that some families discuss the generational wealth among themselves. That is true, I am sure of it. As a matter of fact, I know it to be true. It is a sad truth that some families do not attempt to break free from the cycles that they are stuck in. There has been evidence that wealth and poverty have been passed down from one generation to the next. The types of investments that can be made here are properties, land, money, stocks, bonds, and so on. It is possible to break the cycle of poverty with the right knowledge and management.

It is highly recommended that you refrain from being a part of the family if you see something that you do not want to be a part of. If you want to avoid becoming a gambler, tell yourself, "I will not become one. It is my goal to be a better parent. There will be a college education for me. I am planning on opening my own business or becoming the first homeowner in my family."

It all starts with self-determination, and that is where it all ends.

In terms of the person in the mirror, it has to start somewhere, so where should it begin? Wouldn't it be great if that started with you? The cycle has to be broken by someone at some point.

As soon as my father died, the husband of one of the teachers came to my house to talk with me about working for him. My job was to cut the grass at his house, the church, and the Lodge Hall in Independence, Louisiana. He had no problem using his words to make a point. As a preacher, I guess so, he was known for his sermons. It is not clear to me if he asked me to go to work or told me to come and work. The ethnic characteristics of my own father's work led me to answer, "Yes sir," without hesitating when facing my own question.

It is my understanding that the Bishop knew my father before he passed away and I guess that was his way of supporting my family by providing me with a job. My father was a good provider for his family and the Bishop wanted to make sure that these standards would continue in the future. I worked for him for about five years and then I stopped. He employed my youngest brother Clyde and my nephew as well.

A generational curse can have a major impact on your ability to focus and can cause you to lose focus. As difficult as it can be to break the family curses that cause you to be unable to focus, it is not impossible to do so. Having a clear purpose is one of the most important aspects of being successful and fulfilling your life's purpose. Despite family barriers and hardships, you can overcome them. There is no better time than now to be totally honest with yourself and take a look at your true self.

Take a moment now and write down what you love about your family as well as what you would like to change about your family. What could be generational curses as well as what are your family's strengths?

It is when you change the identifying features that have been a part of your family for generations. What are you going to do to change it and how are you going to do it? What are the steps you will take to get started? In your opinion, why do you think it is so important to change it?

It was very clear to me from the beginning what my benefits were. My parents gave me the foundation that I needed to succeed in life. All I had to do was to keep what was working and change the things that weren't working. Throughout the generations of my family, my parents' teachings have been lost as my family has gotten away from it. I would like to see more love in the family in the future.

Our generation lives in an era of doing me, where everything revolves around the self. The family seems to be getting further and further apart from each other as time goes on. That is when generational focus is almost thrown out of the window if we allow it to be.

I would like to remind you that the only person you can change is yourself. In some cases, there may not be anything that you can do to change the circumstances of your family. However, your life and circumstances can be changed if you decide to do something about them. You are, therefore, changing generations beginning with you by doing so "one generation at a time." You indeed need to have a change of mindset to be successful. It is your responsibility, as it was the responsibility of the Philippians "to keep this mind, which was also in Christ Jesus, within you."

Generational focus can be a useful tool for breaking the cycle of poverty. It is possible to build generational wealth as a result of generational focus. There has to be a beginning of some kind so that it can be passed from one generation to another to survive. You will be able to benefit from it as well as your children and grandchildren. The idea of passing down generational wealth to future generations seems to appeal to everyone. This is yet another time in our lives when we have to take our own narratives of this topic of discussion and change them in our own homes.

It is my hope that this book will help you to open your eyes about yourself. There may be a time when you wonder what family has to do with me. Please do not make the mistake of assuming that it had nothing to do with your success or failure and that family is was totally unrelated. The answer to this question is yes, you must start by helping yourself before you can help anyone else. Yes, you have to help yourself first, and then help the next person in your family. It is important to remember that you cannot help anyone who does not want your help. If they do not wish to be helped, then you are really wasting your time. The fact of the matter is that time is something that cannot be bought back.

A lady I went to school with fell on some hard times due to bad choices she made in her life which led to some bad times in her life. In terms of living conditions, she did not have a good situation. As she looked at me, she said, "I wasn't raised like this, I wasn't brought up like this.". I was taught differently by my parents. It is these choices that I made that I think about on a daily basis. Exactly where I could have been in life if I had followed the blueprints that my parents had written for me when I was growing up. It is not my parents who are at fault in this case, rather it is me.

I know someone who came from a very influential family and they lost focus. I know their parents, they were upstanding citizens.

There was no way that I would have ever guessed that they would have taken such a route. Consequently, they broke the standard their parents set for them. As a result of getting off focus, this is what you end up with at the end. It wasn't like this when they first started. It is now possible for every generation coming behind them to change this foundation if they do not revert to what their mother and father laid down for them many years ago.

If everyone in the family is old enough to understand what is meant by generational focus, then it should be discussed with everyone. We must start somewhere otherwise if we do not start somewhere, we will lose the strength of the family. There are so many things that can be accomplished when a family works collectively together. In my experience, this method has worked over and over again. Matter-of-fact, I know it works.

Currently, I am sixty-four years of age. The family is weakening in our time. This has been a shift in my lifetime. There was a time when I used to see homes with multiple families living in them. Grandparents, parents, uncles, aunts, cousins, and other relatives. It was a team effort and everyone was watching out for each other. It was more common for two parents to live in the same home fifty years ago. The child's life was dominated by the presence of grandparents and other relatives. Those ways of living are being lost to us today. It would be great if we could continue to say that we are seeing generations working together as a team. I mentioned it earlier, but social media has become the family for millions of young people all over the world. It is becoming more and more common for families to talk about how their children are no longer spending time with them. It is the end of the day, and they are in their rooms looking at their cell phones. This topic has been covered in many magazines over the last few years.

It is becoming more and more common for women to raise their children on their own. In some cases, men are not taking on the responsibility of being a father. As a result, children are not being raised around the members of their paternal side of the family. What is the impact of this on family life in the modern world? Even though the child is being raised by a particular branch of the family, the child is still affected by it because it is out of balance. There is no doubt that we are in worse shape today than we were fifty years ago, and it is the result of us not being focused on what we need to do.

The key to success is to get back on track and get back in focus with our families and our community. If we take a look at the families of yesterday, how did they manage to survive? What made these families strong, and why are we seeing a shift in the family nucleus today? Is there anything we can do about it? If you want to break the generational curse of not being able to focus on what is important, then these are the questions you must ask yourself. There is no hope for us until we turn from our wicked ways and get back to God.

> *If my people, who are called by my name, will humble themselves and pray and seek my face and turn from their wicked ways, then I will hear from heaven, and I will forgive their sin and will heal their land.*
>
> *2 Chronicles 7-14*

As for what helps me in my daily life, it is reading my Bible and putting it into practice. I truly believe that it has helped me to remain focused and overcome many challenges. It is very important for everyone to have something that can help them stay focused throughout the day. In the case that you live in a house with other people. There needs to be some time set aside for you to meditate and focus. There are twenty-four hours in a day. The only thing you are asking for is twenty minutes each day to meditate and practice focusing. The more you do this, the easier it will be for you to make it a habit. You should not be afraid to break old habits and replace them with new habits that are better suited to your purpose and mission and will help you achieve your goals more effectively.

It has been a long and arduous process of writing and editing my book, but it was all well worth it. It is a fact that I am certain of. Furthermore,

 The purpose of this book is to heal you, to help you to cut out some of the distractions, that keep you from being able to focus on what is important to you. It will help you understand how important it is to cut off distractions that can take you out of focus. There could be a need to cut off a friend or relative who is draining your mental energy. Eliminate bad habits that are holding you back and develop new habits that will help you achieve your goals.

Some people are very easily influenced by their surroundings. There is no doubt that peer pressure is a real issue. It doesn't matter how old you are. There is no doubt that we are easily influenced by others. There are two ways in which this can be viewed, either positively or negatively. My sincere hope is that the people around you are influencing you positively.

My family would eat dinner together every night, and everyone talked about the events of the day at school, as well as the tasks at hand. The importance of family meetings and discussions can be taught to children through the communication. It can help them learn the skills of discussing issues and constructively resolving problems. This is a great opportunity for them to learn how to focus on the subject and that will be of great benefit to them in the future as well.

The challenge maybe getting them to sit at the table. We must be creative if we are going to work on developing a generational focus. It is a good idea to call a meeting and write down the agenda. Keep in mind that it does not have to be a long agenda for the family meeting. Ideally, it can start by discussing the importance of family meetings and the benefits that can be derived from them. To sum it up, it's all about getting them interested in the lives of each family member.

The movie "Soul Food" comes to mind when I think of Big Mama's mission on Sundays which was to gather all her children and grandchildren around the dinner table. It was a challenge, and that is a challenge that many families face today as well. Nowadays everyone is doing different things and going their own way, and there is little time for the family to spend time together. Oftentimes, children don't visit their parents like they used to as often as they used to. They made sure that they would come home during the holidays if they lived away from home. It was the Sundays after church in rural communities that were like family reunions in and of themselves. There were many times when the family ate together, and we would have visitors come over.

There are several ways in which families can communicate with one another in the 21st century, such as Zoom, Facebook, and Face-

Time. This is especially true for those who live outside of the state. There is no better way to stay in touch with family than this.

The main point is for everyone to stay in contact with one another and build strong family ties as I did as a child growing up in a small town of Independence, Louisiana. There is a sense of community in small towns because everyone knows everybody. Somehow, we all had a distant relationship with one another. It can be through marriage or long-term friendships that have felt like family for many years.

QUESTIONS

1. Define generational focus. _____
   _____
   _____

2. Why do you think that generational focus is important? _____
   _____
   _____

3. How has generational focus impacted on your life?
   _____
   _____

4. What is the good impact of generational focus in your life? ___
   _____
   _____

5. What is the bad impact of generational focus in your life? ___
   _____
   _____

6. What can you do to change the negative impact? _____
   _____
   _____

7. When will you start? _____

DISTRACTIONS AND PROCRASTINATION

When it comes to distractions, it can be problems that come up frequently as a result of a variety of factors that may or may not be beyond your control. Imagine you are going to work in the morning and everything is fine on your part. You arrive at work and find that one of your coworkers is having a bad day, and they are blaming it on you. As soon as you can, you need to eliminate this distraction.

Regardless of the mundane things of life, we encounter every day, they do not serve as a distraction from the fact that we have to get up every day to go to work, get the kids off to school, and take care of our families. Every day, it happens in some form or another. It is important to remember, however, that some distractions are beyond your control. Consequently, you must deal with it day to day. Even if it's two or three things going on the same day, you have to address it at the point whenever it arises. I suggest you remain calm and stay focused. Think the process out and stay on track.

You got up early to prepare for work, you woke up early and got the kids up for school, and you found time to meditate that morning. You had your day arranged, and almost everything was working out the way you wanted it to. However, something comes up that distracts from what you already have in mind. To succeed, you must be able to handle it in a way that helps you achieve your goals or purpose.

In other words, you know the difference. You know what to do in those situations, and you know the difference between mundane routines. In this regard, since things aren't going according to plan, it is easy to see the difference between the two.

In an episode of The Ricky Smiley Show, the hosts and guests discussed social media and the amount of time we spend on it. It was also discussed how it can be used as a means of distraction from our everyday lives. The point that Ricky Smiley was referring to is how much we are distracted by social media and it hinders our progress. I believe it is my goal in my book to eliminate as much wasted time and energy as possible especially when it comes to social media.

It is common for us to be distracted by things such as divorce, job loss, and the death of a loved one. We must remember that life will continue to carry on, so we should be aware of how far we allow those distractions to take us offline. Many distractions can be avoided by not becoming involved in other people's business, because most of the time, what happens with other people has nothing to do with us. We are able to eliminate that one big distraction by the fact that you have twelve hours in a day to mind your own business, and twelve hours in a day to leave someone else's business alone. Getting involved in other's business is a major distraction that you should avoid at all costs.

In fact, you should avoid getting involved in anything that has nothing to do with you. During my everyday life, I know that I have to exercise great caution when doing electrical work since my job is quite dangerous. As a result, I need to eliminate every distraction that I can control as well as any distraction that does not concern me while I am on the job. If I allow someone or something to distract me, I may harm myself and others. Not to mention the possibility of causing a fatal electrical fire.

What is the difference between a controlled distraction and an out-of-control distraction? If something comes up in your life that doesn't have anything to do with you, then, you can control it and you don't have to get involved. You have the out-of-control thing directly hitting you, you can't avoid it, and you have to deal with it, but then you have to keep the distraction to a minimum so that you can get back to your goal and purpose.

The ability to deal with distractions is crucial. Identifying the distraction or problem is the first step in improving the situation. I would like to suggest that you start by identifying an area where you need to improve to move forward. The second most significant step is a change of mind.

> *Let this mind also be in you that was also in Christ Jesus.*
>
> Philippians 2:5

Before anything can be achieved, there must first be a mindset change. This is a very crucial step in the process. Identifying what is taking you off course and then realizing, "I have to change because this is taking me off course. I am not focused." So, your first step should be identifying what needs to be changed.

Self-responsibility is essential. We often say this in church, and it's true, we inflict a lot of wounds on ourselves. We lose focus. I've done it to myself, I've lost focus. Due to self-inflicted damage, I had to get back on track. In this book, you will learn how to identify what is holding you back from your purpose and goals. Previously, I stated that we have more control over our lives than we admit to. If we want to reach our purpose and goals in life, we need to take an inventory of ourselves and strive to become better individuals.

It's overwhelming to see everything that is going on in the world, and we just have to identify what does not concern us and let it go. We have so much that distracts us these days: we're watching television, we're watching the political scene, we're watching the sports scene, we've got our favorite team, we don't like what happened with this particular person, that particular politician—all of that is distracting. It is also important to watch television with an open mind. There is no way to close your mind and focus on only one thing at a time, you will get distracted and lose focus. The importance of minimizing your focus in order to maximize your performance cannot be overstated.

Once we identify our individual problem, we can minimize it, eliminate what does not concern us, and then work towards the goal we are trying to achieve. As I mentioned earlier, you should always improve your lifestyle even if you do not have a specific goal in mind. It doesn't matter what you're working on, whether you're working on a goal or a task. The bottom line is everyone wants to improve their personal life. The first step to begin this process is to eliminate what does not concern you. If you can, think of one good thing that happened to you in your life, then think of one thing that happened to you that you regret because you did not stay focused or because you were distracted.

To be successful in my electrical business, I believe that staying focused is key. It was important for me to maintain a good credit history, to have a certain amount of cash in the bank, to prove that I am working every day, and to have insurance coverage.

Despite the outside chatter, I did not allow myself to be distracted by the people who told me how hard starting a business would be. I had to stay focused and follow the state's requirements, the parish's requirements, and the city's requirements because they are all different. My paperwork had to be organized and accurate in order for me to get it done. My finances had to be in order in order to accomplish this.

Just like writing this book, another dream came true because I followed the instructions that were given to me. My friend who became one of the consultants informed me of the steps I had to take to start my business. I followed his instructions and my dream came true. When I decided to start my business, I had to obtain insurance, permits, and licenses, and had to have my finances in order. Melvin McElwee, a very good friend of mine, was my mentor, motivator, and a positive influence during that time. He gave me phone numbers, and he told me who to contact for assistance and opportunities to enhance my work. There was a process involved. I couldn't do it in my current state, but I was able to accomplish it once I took all of these steps one at a time. I had a few distractions, but I eliminated them once I found them. That's how we alleviated the distractions by doing the process step by step. There were challenges, but I had to follow the process to get to my goal. Everything flowed so smoothly after I did that, and it worked beautifully.

It was my goal to minimize distractions as much as possible. When it came to my determination to become a business owner, I did not allow anything to distract me from my goal. The moment my friend, McElwee, explained to me what had to be done, my distraction was eliminated and my focus was maximized. In order to achieve what I needed to accomplish, the process had begun. Everything just fell into place due to me taking the initiative and taking action. Because I didn't know the steps to business ownership, it would have been impossible for me to accomplish anything without my dear friend's help and guidance. This will be the same for you to reach your goal. Surround yourself with people who can help you achieve your purpose and goal.

There was a lot of time spent studying for tests, completing forms, and reviewing documents. I knew that time would be of the essence if I was to accomplish what I needed to accomplish. Alternatively, if

I were to put it another way, everything had to be done to reach the goal. I had to remove some people from my life to achieve my goal. I needed to make this decision, so please understand that I was forced to do so. It would be ideal for me to work with people that understand what I'm trying to accomplish and who will help me achieve it.

We talked about the fact that I was unable to go out with my friends and associates. Unfortunately, I could not join them on several nights out. To study for my exams, I had to make time for such, even if that meant knocking off work earlier that day. There was a need for me to focus all of my attention on studying for my exams as well as completing the paperwork. After sixteen years, I can look back and say that I succeeded in my mission. It is therefore my intention to encourage you to do the same.

It is critical that you identify distractions and avoiding them. A major distraction can come in a variety of forms, and only you have the ability to determine what they are. Your choice is to either continue allowing unwanted distractions to keep you from reaching your goals, or you can choose to ignore them. Alternatively, you can remove them from your life completely. For example, if you change your mind while writing a paper, you will be able to delete a word or sentence. When dealing with distractions, you should follow the same approach as if you deleted a sentence or word.

There are three things that people do in their lives. Whether they are rich, or poor. Every person looks at the past, the present, and where they're going for the future. Therefore, we sometimes just have to stand still and reflect on where we are in our lives. In order to continue where we are going, we must observe whether we were able to stay focused or if we need to become more focused for us to make progress.

I think it is very important for me to talk about procrastination and how it affects people. There is no doubt that procrastination can distract you from the goal that you are attempting to achieve. Procrastination should be minimized as much as possible. Procrastination can lead to many unnecessary problems in our lives. Whenever possible, avoid procrastination. It's human nature to procrastinate from time to time. The practice should not become habitual, however.

It is easy to become overwhelmed when we procrastinate. If you do not pay your utility bill by the due date, you will be charged a late fee. It's not that you don't have the money, it's just that you didn't pay your bill on time. Firstly, your services can be disconnected, secondly, you can spend unnecessary money if you pay your bill late because of procrastination.

If I procrastinate by not returning phone calls to my customers as a business owner, it can make me lose credibility, money, and potential clients. Procrastination is often associated with laziness and fatigue. It is important to remember that procrastination does come at a price. The bottom line is that it always does, no matter what.

It is common for some people to blame others for their life circumstances. Throughout my life, I have never blamed anyone, because I know what happened to me was self-inflicted. This is a fact I am certain of. I have overcome some bad things in life that were caused by choices and procrastination. My actions did not deter me, it was my own fault. We all have to make individual choices. Those choices will determine our success or failure.

The importance of procrastination cannot be overstated, for it determines success or failure. Due to my awareness of procrastination. It is something I try to avoid at all costs. To accomplish my daily tasks and stay on top of my schedule, I must avoid it. Procrastination cannot stand in the way of my goals. I have a lot of responsibilities. Some employees rely on me for their livelihood. When it comes to achieving your goals, procrastination is not an option. To achieve my goals, I must stay focused and not give in to procrastination.

Focusing and avoiding distractions are two things I challenge myself to do. There is a limit to everything. Clint Eastwood once said, "Every man needs to know his limitations." Therefore, what he is saying you need to know your limitation. What I'm teaching here is how to recognize and limit those distractions. Procrastination is a distraction.

QUESTIONS

1. Define procrastination. _____
_____
_____

2. How have you experienced procrastination? _____
_____
_____

3. How can you avoid procrastination?
_____
_____
_____

4. Are you easily distracted? _____
_____
_____

5. What are something that distract you? _____
_____
_____

6. What can you to do control your distractions?
_____
_____
_____

7. Does distractions and procrastination keeping you from achieving your goals and purpose? _____

_____

_____

8. What are you willing to do to change procrastination and distractions? _____

_____

YOU ARE ON YOUR WAY

I hope you have enjoyed reading the book and answered the questions that have been provided at the end of each chapter. It is my sincere hope that you have gained a great deal of knowledge about yourself as a result of this experience. There is no doubt in my mind that we all have goals, dreams, and tasks that we want to accomplish, and many times we need help to do so. It may be impossible for you to achieve your goals and dreams without a plan of action. Throughout the previous chapters, I have repeatedly stated that the only person who is able to determine what it is that you have to lose or gain is you.

At the end of the day, I hope that you learn to remain focused and keep your eyes on your prize at all times. I believe that it is important for you to remember that you are ready for a change, and that change does not happen in a vacuum. After reading this book, you should have a clear understanding of yourself. What your goals are and the vision that you have in mind. Having a clear mental state mind is very important.

As you become more self-aware, you are able to gain a better understanding of who are and what it takes to accomplish your goals. As a result, you are able to identify changes that you need to make as well as your own strengths that you can build on as you move forward with your goals. Having a strong sense of self-awareness is often the first step in setting goals. As part of this, you need to admit when you do not know the answer and accept responsibility for your mistakes, and weakness. Once again we all face the same situations when trying to accomplish our goals.

I wish I could tell you tell you there is an easier way, however, life doesn't afford us that. It just doesn't work way. I learned throughout the years, there is no short cut. I had to travel the journey of up and downs, mundane things of life like any other person who wanted to accomplish a goal or task.

I wish I could tell you that there is a simpler way to do things, but life doesn't provide us with that opportunity. It just doesn't work that way. Over the years, I have learned that there is no shortcut to success. As with any person who wishes to accomplish a certain goal or task in their life, I had to go through the same journey of ups and downs, mundane things of life as anyone else who wishes to accomplish a certain goal or task in their life.

There is no doubt that staying focused and not giving up is the best way to succeed. You can achieve success if you follow the steps and principles outlined in this book. Upon reflection, you will realize that this was one of the best investments you could have made for yourself. It is a self-help book that is intended to assist you in achieving your goals.

Before now, I must be completely honest and say that I did not read any self-help books on the topic. My writing is based on my own experiences. After I began writing my own book. It was as if we were inside each other's minds when I read some of the other authors' works on the subject. They books talked the mundane things of life and many of the same subjects I outlined in my very own book.

I believe that "great minds think alike" and now, my book will be included among those who wish to assist others in achieving their goals. We can't do it for you, but we can help you stay focused. In order to achieve your goals, you need to change your mindset, and this can be the key to success. It is likely that you will have to read the book more than once in order to absorb all of the information in it.

I was reading Proverb 23:7, "For as he thinkers in his heart, so is he: Eat and drink, saith he to thee; but his heart is not with thee."

Everyone wants to be successful, no one wants to fail. There may be a lack of knowledge about how to achieve success. It is common for people to fail without knowing why. I hope the formula in my book helps you succeed. Most of us don't try because we're afraid of failing. Success comes from failure. If you're reading this book, you're ready to elevate yourself.

Are you ready to take the journey to new discoveries and success that awaits you? Because you are holding this book in your hands, I am confident that you are aware of what it says. As I listened to Earl Nightingale's audio book, *As a Man Thinketh*, which was recorded by James Allen, he says the greatest mistake in life is giving up. He also speaks about the journey of the mind and where it can take you. How do you see yourself, where do you want to see yourself? Just remember the man or woman in the mirror is the only person who holds the keys.